THE BOOK OF
DALS

ADVANCE PRAISE FOR *THE BOOK OF DALS*

'Following the successful publication of her earlier books on Hyderabadi cuisine and Biryani, Pratibha Karan once again brings out a stunning cookbook—*The Book of Dals*.

'With her background that includes a very rewarding IAS career and induction into a Hyderabadi aristocratic family, this book is a little different from the previous ones that had a fair touch of hedonistic culinary pleasures. From the table of emperors and kings to the daily wage worker of today, dal is ubiquitous and has endeared all through the ages.

'Displaying a high level of personal knowledge and painstaking effort, Pratibha Karan takes you on a tour of our country's various regions capturing the diverse flavours of dals.

'With my personal knowledge when dining at her home where dishes were prepared by her to everyone's great delight, the recipes of her choice here are sure to provide immense joy to all those cooking and savouring them. Enriched with beautiful photographs, this book is a celebration of dals.'

HABIB REHMAN,
Former Director, ITC
Hotels, Foods, Travel and Tourism

THE BOOK OF
DALS

PRATIBHA KARAN

EBURY
PRESS

An imprint of Penguin Random House

EBURY PRESS

USA | Canada | UK | Ireland | Australia
New Zealand | India | South Africa | China

Ebury Press is part of the Penguin Random House group of companies
whose addresses can be found at global.penguinrandomhouse.com

Published by Penguin Random House India Pvt. Ltd
4th Floor, Capital Tower 1, MG Road,
Gurgaon 122 002, Haryana, India

First published in Ebury Press by Penguin Random House India 2022

Photography by Shumaila Chauhan
Food styling by Nikita Rao
Author's photograph by Amit Vadehra
Book design by Sanchita Mukherjee
Crockery and cutlery courtesy
Nicobar, Good Earth, Gigi Chakra, Le Creuset and Ellementry

ISBN 9780670092178

Typeset in Futura LT Pro type family by Sanchita Mukherjee
Printed at Replika Press Pvt. Ltd, India

www.penguin.co.in

For Azaan—
our first grandchild and the
joy of our lives

CONTENTS

FOREWORD

I first met Pratibha Karan and her husband, Vijay Karan, in 2009 when I was posted to New Delhi as the interim American ambassador, awaiting the arrival of President Obama's nominee. And again in 2011–12, when I was in Delhi on another, much longer, assignment. I should be embarrassed to confess that I met Pratibha Karan when, as a result of reading and using her extraordinary cookbook, *A Princely Legacy: Hyderabadi Cuisine*, I called her out of the blue and more or less invited myself to dinner. She, being incredibly courteous, replied with an invitation and made me feel that she had actually initiated the gesture, and not the opposite.

On the night of the dinner, there was some confusion in my embassy's office and we thought I was invited for 7 p.m., though that seemed remarkably early for an Indian dinner. Being an American, I arrived on time and found no one was expecting me. In fact, my shouting at the entryway to the house panicked the Karans' two daughters, Gauri and Nainika, who shrieked and fled to their rooms! Pratibha Karan appeared, obviously not ready to be hosting a dinner, but greeted me with aplomb anyway and ushered me into the cosy living room. In a few moments, Vijay Karan appeared and Pratibha excused herself to prepare for the dinner. As the lively conversation with Vijay gathered momentum, gradually, Gauri, Nainika and Karans' son, Gaurav, appeared, joining in and enabling their father to excuse himself to also get ready to host the evening.

Thus, began a twelve-year relationship with the entire Karan family—Pratibha and Vijay, their three children, their children's spouses and their children—which continues to this day, whenever I am in India or they come to the US. And, during this time, there were many scrumptious dinners, planned and orchestrated by Pratibha.

I regularly use both the *Hyderabadi Cuisine* and, then later, Pratibha's *Biryani* cookbooks and have been avidly testing many of the dal recipes in this new book over the past six months. How Pratibha managed to collect these recipes from all over India plus Sri Lanka, Nepal and Pakistan is a mystery to me, but she has done it. Her network of friends throughout the subcontinent shared treasured family recipes. And she clearly and succinctly gives each recipe thoughtful descriptions and directions which are easy to follow—and the dishes are marvellous. As I was new to Sindhi cuisine, I found those recipes particularly intriguing. And, having spent many years in Colombo and Kathmandu, I was happy to see authentic Sri Lankan and Nepali recipes included in this compendium of delicacies.

My guess is that most readers of this book will be surprised at the variety and uniqueness of the many regional variations of dal preparations detailed, from Jammu & Kashmir in the far north to Kerala and Tamil Nadu in the south. It is astonishing to see how regional culinary styles and history infuse each of these dishes with special flavours and results, often with the same lentil as base but with local creativity using ingredients and spices preferred and available.

Dals are consumed by all social classes in India and are an important source of protein. It is unusual to have any meal in India without dal and what Pratibha Karan has done with this important book is to open our eyes to the vast array of delicious variations on these lentils.

Both Indians and foreigners like myself who savour Indian food owe a huge debt of gratitude to Pratibha Karan for the years of research and discovery that have clearly gone into this effort. This book is a must for anyone seriously interested in Indian cuisine.

A. Peter Burleigh
US Ambassador (retired)
Fort Lauderdale, Florida, USA

INTRODUCTION

Dals are an integral part of Indian cuisine. They are prepared in most homes, every day, as just a simple dish or a part of a more elaborate meal. And each region, according to its taste and availability of ingredients, embellishes dals by adding fish, meat, coconut milk, cream, vegetables and a host of aromatic spices.

Craving for a heart-warming dal, if you are away from home, is simply natural. In Hyderabad, when people return from travels and are asked what they would like to eat, the answer is, 'Khatti dal and chawal'.

To quote Vir Sanghvi, a noted journalist and a renowned food critic:

> Dal is the great unifier of all Indian cuisines. Nearly everywhere you go in India, you will find dal on the thali or the plate. It could be the dal fry, so popular at dhabas in north India. It could be the slightly sweet cholar dal [Bengal gram lentils, split and skinned] that is so distinctively Bengali. It could be the many complex sambars of the South Indian states. Or it could be the amazing sweet-sour tuvar dal [red gram lentils] that is at the heart of Gujarati cuisine. So dal is not just an important part of Indian food. In many ways, it is Indian food. It is the defining dish of Indian cuisine.[1]

Now, something about legumes, lentils and pulses.

Legumes are plants whose seeds are enclosed in a pod. There are two types of legumes—mature and immature. Mature legumes are dried seeds found inside pods that hang from the stem of certain plants. Green beans and peas, commonly referred to as vegetables, are immature legumes because they are harvested before they mature. Legumes include peas, beans, peanuts, pulses, chickpeas, dried beans, dried peas and lentils. Lentils are also treated as part of pulses. In India, lentils and pulses are broadly referred to as 'dal' in Hindi.

Lentils/pulses have been an essential part of the human diet for centuries. They are an affordable alternative to more expensive, animal-based protein foods and ideal for improving diets and adding variety to a vegetarian's diet. Lentils have high nutritional

---

[1] *Virsanghvi.com*

value. They are low in fat, and high in protein and fibre. Most varieties provide half our foliate requirement. They are a good source of phosphorous, potassium, iron, magnesium, zinc and calcium. They also help regulate blood glucose levels, reduce cholesterol and lower blood pressure.

Lentils have a mild and often earthy and nutty flavour. They can be cooked with assertive flavouring. There are many enticing varieties of lentils to choose from. Some are described below:

- *Bengal gram lentils, whole (kala chana)*—These lentils are rust-coloured with a nutty flavour.
- *Bengal gram lentils, split and skinned (chana dal)*—These lentils are canary yellow in colour, and rich in flavour.
- *Black gram lentils, whole (urad dal, sabut)*—These lentils have a black skin and creamy white interior. They derive their strong and earthy flavour from the black skin.
- *Black gram lentils, split and skinned (urad dal, dhuli)*— These lentils are much milder in taste than urad dal (sabut).
- *Black gram lentils, split and unskinned (urad dal, dali)*—These lentils are milder in taste than urad dal (sabut).
- *Ochre lentils, whole (masoor dal, sabut).*
- *Orange or pink lentils, also known as red lentils, split and skinned (masoor dal, dhuli).*
- *Red gram lentils (arhar dal).*
- *Green gram lentils, whole (moong dal, sabut).*
- *Green gram lentils, skinned and split (moong dal, dhuli)*—They have a yellow hue. It is also referred to as yellow lentils.
- *Green gram lentils, unskinned and split (moong dal, dali).*
- *Chickpeas (Kabuli chana).*
- *Red kidney beans (rajma)*—Rich maroon-red beans, which are rich in flavour and ever so mildly sweet.
- *Black-eyed beans (lobia).*

These are just some of the lentils that are found in India today. The variety of dals and other dishes that can be cooked with these lentils is phenomenal and mind-boggling. India is the world's largest producer and consumer of lentils/pulses. Pakistan, Canada, Myanmar, Australia and the US, in that order, are significant exporters and are suppliers of pulses for India. Pulses are consumed more in India than anywhere else in the world.

Under the slogan, 'Nutritious seeds for a sustainable future', the UN, led by its Food and Agriculture Organization (FAO), launched the year 2016 as the 'Year of Pulses'[2] to raise awareness about the power of protein in pulses and their health benefits, and boost their production and trade.

Lentils are used throughout south and west Asia and the Mediterranean region. They

---

[2] *The 68th United Nations General Assembly (UNGA) declared year 2016 as the International Year of Pulses (IYP)*

are frequently combined with rice. A dal and rice dish in Arab countries is referred to as mujaddara or mejadre. A similar dish called kushari, is made in Egypt and is considered one of the two national dishes.

Majorcan Chickpea Soup is a rustic soup, thick with vegetables, which is sold in the back streets of Palma, Spain. The Lebanese Lentil Soup is made with ochre lentils combined with a variety of vegetables like carrots, potatoes and spinach.

Lentils are used to prepare an inexpensive and nutritious soup all over Europe and North and South America, sometimes combined with chicken or pork.

The Greek Bean Soup is made with haricot beans in combination with tomatoes, celery, parsley and bay leaf. In Mexico, dishes made with kidney beans and minced meat (keema) are a part of the staple diet. Then we have the Swedish Yellow Pea Soup, which is prepared with yellow peas and ham.

In Italy, sausages and meat are prepared with haricot beans, and enjoyed. Boston is famous for its Baked Beans and Pork dish. In Texas and Mexico, many lovely dishes are made using minced meat and kidney beans.

In India, dals are enjoyed in myriad ways. A simple dish of dal or khichri is a breeze to make and the epitome of comfort food. And the spicy and tantalizing preparations, such as the Khatti Dal of Hyderabad, flavoured with tamarind and red chillies, are just as enticing for people.

In Kerala, various dals are made along with vegetables, such as French beans, carrots and cabbage, and are seasoned with red chillies and curry leaves. Most dishes are flavoured with a host of aromatic spices such as cloves, green cardamoms, cinnamon and fennel seeds, and with green chillies and shallots. Coconut is used in various dishes in many different forms (desiccated, cubed and so on).

Maharashtrian dals, such as Moong Usal and Katachi Amti, are made with red gram lentils, moth beans and chickpeas. These dishes are characterized by using ingredients such as peanuts, sugar or jaggery, asafoetida, green chillies, fresh green coriander and of course, coconut and lime.

Some exotic Sindhi dishes include Tidali—a mix of three dals and sawa saag—which is a dal made with spinach, green gourd, etc. Then we have the famous Sindhi Dal Curry made using arhar dal and cooked with either with a host of vegetables or just the gypsy beans. The dish is normally served with rice. It is a favourite of ours and finds place of pride on our table as part of lunch on Sundays. It is usually served along with fried potatoes called Took. We often refer to it as 'Sunday Curry'.

Hyderabad is known for its extensive use of souring agents and red chillies. So, typically, dals are often flavoured with tamarind or lime juice and red chillies using a variety of vegetables such as fresh fenugreek, drumsticks, tomatoes, kairi and chigur (the tender shoots of tamarind). Several green vegetables are also used in combination with lentils such as spinach and ambada. For example, Chigur Chane ki Dal is as dainty in taste as the soft, fragrant and gently sour tamarind shoots. These dals are truly tantalizing.

West Bengal specializes in cooking dals with desiccated coconut, raisin and cashew nuts, along with whole spices, ghee and sugar. Frequently, fish is added to the lentils.

The northern states offer Pindi Chole, Maa ki Dal, Rajma and Dal Tarka. No festive occasion is complete in Rajasthan without its famed Dal Baati Churma, which is prepared using a mix of five different dals, seasoned with spices and liberal use of ghee.

From Kashmir, we have the famous Rajma and the flavourful Arhar Dal aur Shalgam.

Bisi Bele Huliyana is a phenomenal dish from Karnataka, in which dals are cooked with rice and vegetables and flavoured with spices such as fennel seeds, coriander seeds, aniseeds and seasoned with ghee, dry red chillies and curry leaves. Dhansak is an exotic Parsi dish and is made from masoor dal and arhar dal together with fenugreek leaves, brinjals, tomatoes and flavoured with a host of spices. To quote Vir Sanghvi, again, 'Dhansak is the greatest dal and meat dish ever invented anywhere in the world.'[3] There are of course so many mind-blowing versions of this dish, including one made with meat.

During the month of Ramazan, many street-side eateries spring up in Hyderabad, selling Haleem that is made essentially with meat or chicken, along with broken wheat and lentils. It is very popular amongst the Muslim community of the Malabar region. It is also served as breakfast in Arab homes, especially in the Barkas area of Hyderabad near Char Minar.

A combination of meat, dals and broken wheat, Khichra is another amazing dish. It is a variation of Haleem and is particularly popular, but not restricted to, the Muslim community of South Asia. The dish is also popular among the Bohra community in western India.

Dal is ubiquitous. It is used to make all manner of savoury dishes and treats, such as papads, vadas, idlis, dosa, sambar, sun dried vadis, dal moth, sprouts and soups. It is also used in desserts of different kinds such as Moong Dal ka Halwa or Khajoor ka Halwa (prepared using dates with chana dal).

Dried lentils and pulses like moong dal (sabut), kala chana, lobia or moth dal are sprouted by rinsing them, soaking them in water overnight and keeping them covered in a moist, coarse cloth for 2–3 days. They are a delightful and nutritious addition to salads and soups.

---

[3] *Virsanghvi.com*

Dal is generally rinsed and soaked in deep water for about 20–30 minutes or, sometimes, overnight before being cooked. Soaking dal before cooking rehydrates them and they cook evenly and more completely. Soaking also helps in reducing the flatulence. Besides, it allows for shorter cooking time, saves fuel and preserves nutrients. So, you get the benefits of all the proteins, vitamins and minerals, and maximize the nutritional value of dal.

Dal can be pressure cooked or cooked in a pan, partly covered. As a cardinal rule, the water used while cooking is generally 2½ to 3 times the volume of dal. For example, if you are cooking 1 cup of masoor or arhar dal you will need to add 2½ to 3 glasses of water. If you are pressure cooking the dal of the quantity of water can be reduced by half a glass.

Dal should be cooked till just about tender. If you are using a pressure cooker, usually they should be cooked till just 1–2 whistles before turning off the flame. Do not open the pressure cooker till the steam subsides, as the dal will cook further in the steam captured in the pressure cooker.

Cooking without pressure, in a heavy pan partly/fully covered will take a little longer. We need to ensure that when done, dal should not be overcooked and must not become mushy. Again, if there is excess water when done, it can be boiled away; and if the lentils are not tender enough, a little warm water can be added to cook the dal further till tender. Some dals take longer to cook, such as, black lentils, rajma, black gram lentils or chickpeas. These, therefore, require longer soaking time, preferably overnight. These can then be cooked till 2–3 whistles and then further cooked on a low flame for another 8–10 minutes. Some varieties of dals are light and mild, and cook quickly like masoor dal (sabut and dhuli) and arhar dal. These can easily be cooked without pressure.

A magical thing that infuses dals with flavour is the 'baghar' or seasoning. Once cooked, you sizzle a handful of spices in hot ghee or oil and add to the cooked dal. This transforms the dish and makes it taste sublime. Ghee always lends that extra flavour. The spice-blend varies depending on the dish. There is a vast number of ingredients to choose from like mustard seed, cumin seeds, fennel and also whole spices, such as cloves, cardamom, cinnamon, bay leaf, caraway seeds and many more aromatic spices. As soon as the baghar is ready and added to the dish, immediately cover the lid so that the essence and the aroma of the spices, drawn out by hot ghee or oil, is infused into the dish.

An important thing to remember is that there are no rules to cooking. Cooking is about creativity. One can seize upon the immediately available ingredients and work wonders.

Cooking connects you to family, friends and traditions. It's about love and nurturing the loved ones. It's about reinforcing warmth and tenderness. What joy to see your family and loved ones eating in raptures and your dining room filled with laughter, smiles and happiness. So, here we go. Let's try with dals.

DALS

ARHAR DAL

Red gram lentils

URAD DAL, DALI

Black gram lentils,
split and unskinned

KABULI CHANA

Chickpeas

URAD DAL, DHULI

Black gram lentils,
split and skinned

RAJMA

Red Kidney beans

MASOOR DAL, DHULI

Red lentils, split
and skinned

MOONG DAL, SABUT

Green gram
lentils, whole

MATAR

Dry Peas

URAD DAL, SABUT

Black gram
lentils, whole

KALA CHANA

Bengal gram
lentils, whole

CHANA DAL

Bengal gram lentils,
split and skinned

LOBIA

Black-eyed beans

MOONG DAL, DHULI

Green gram lentils,
split and skinned

MASOOR DAL, SABUT

Ochre lentils

A NOTE FOR THE READER

Cooking is a creative art. While wonderful results can be achieved by following formal recipes, you can always play around with available ingredients and it can work gloriously.

As this book essentially deals with dals, I would like to explain briefly about the terminology used in the book. Pulses are part of lentils. Lentils and pulses are broadly referred to in Hindi as 'dals'. Lentils and pulses belong to the legume family. Legumes are plants whose seeds are enclosed in a pod.

DALS

There are several varieties of dals to choose from. They are rinsed and soaked in deep water generally for about 20–30 minutes before cooking. However, some lentils require longer soaking and cooking time. For example, black lentils (urad dal, sabut), Bengal gram lentils, whole (kala chana) and red kidney beans (rajma) need to be soaked overnight and preferably cooked in a pressure cooker. Some other lentils are light and take much less soaking and cooking time. For example, red lentils (masoor dal, dhuli), red gram lentil (arhar dal), green gram lentils skinned and split (moong dal, dhuli). These dals can easily be cooked in a normal heavy-base pan without pressure. Water used while cooking is generally 2½ to 3 times the volume of the lentils. Pressure cooking the lentils will require lesser quantity of water and will take lesser time i.e. if you are cooking 1 cup of lentils, 3 cups of water will be required if cooking without pressure. The quantity of water can be reduced to 2½ cups, if using pressure cooker. One thing to be kept in mind, however, is that overcooking the lentils tends to ruin its flavour.

SEASONING

Seasoning is something that embellishes a dish and enhances its flavours.
Once the lentils are cooked, you can sizzle a handful of spices in hot ghee or oil and add them to the dish. It transforms and enriches the flavours of the dish. After adding seasoning to the dals, covering it immediately with a lid helps to infuse the flavours

into the dish and capture its aroma. Ghee, of course, adds the extra flavour. Seasoning in Hindi is also referred to as baghar, tarka and chonk which are all the same.

SPICES GENERALLY USED IN SEASONING

The variety of spices available in India is vast. However, some essential spices that are used to season lentils once they are cooked include dry red chillies, cinnamon sticks, fenugreek seeds, mustard seeds, cumin seeds, cardamom and asafoetida. Chopped onions, chopped ginger and garlic, green chillies (chopped or whole), chopped tomatoes are also often used in seasoning.
Any small or medium sized pan will do for seasoning.

OIL

Normally any good commercially available vegetable oil can be used in cooking unless otherwise specified such as olive oil, mustard oil or coconut oil. These oils are derived from different sources such as sunflower, sesame, ground nut, peanut, corn, soya bean, mustard, olive, coconut, etc.

GHEE

Ghee is clarified butter.

HOW TO BLANCH TOMATOES

To blanch 5–6 tomatoes, wash them and plunge the tomatoes into boiling water for about 2–3 minutes till the skin breaks at a few places. Take out the tomatoes and run them under cold water for a few seconds. Peel off the skin and chop roughly. Use them as required.

HOW TO EXTRACT TAMARIND JUICE

To extract juice from 100 g tamarind, wash and soak the tamarind in 1½ glasses of hot water for about 15–20 minutes. Soaking longer will only make the tamarind softer, making it easier to extract the tamarind juice. Mash them with hands over a sieve to extract the tamarind juice. Discard the seeds and residue.

Tamarind juice can be extracted in larger quantity and stored in the deep freeze and used whenever needed. This will remain fresh in the deep freeze for 2–3 weeks.

HOW TO EXTRACT COCONUT MILK

Take out the kernel of 1 coconut. Either grate or chop the coconut. Add 1½ glasses of water and churn it in a mixie. Tie the mixture in a muslin cloth and squeeze with your hands to extract coconut milk. Alternatively, you could also sieve the mixture through a strainer to extract coconut milk. The quantity of coconut can be adjusted according to the requirement of the recipe.

HOW TO USE GREEN CHILLIES

Green chillies can be chopped, slit or hard broken into two, and added to the dish. Green chillies can also be split into two vertically or they can be slit on one side slightly down the line and then added to the dish.

SALT

The quantity of salt to be used is a matter of personal preference. I have, therefore, left it open to the reader to use salt as per taste. However, generally speaking, if you are cooking 250 g of lentils about 1 tsp (not heaped) salt can be added.

WATER MEASUREMENT

An average sized glass can hold 250 ml/8.5 ounces of water.

OIL MEASUREMENT

100 g vegetable oil = 108.53 ml (rounded off to 110 ml) vegetable oil.

I cup vegetable oil = Approx. 200 ml vegetable oil
½ cup vegetable oil = Approx. 100 ml vegetable oil
¼ cup vegetable oil = Approx. 50 ml vegetable oil.

And finally, whatever you cook, do it with confidence and aplomb and serve triumphantly.

REGIONAL INTRODUCTION

India, with twenty-eight states and nine union territories, has diverse food cultures. Religion, traditions and customs all impact the food of a particular region.

Foreign invasions, foreign rules, colonization, trade relations and immigration have all played an important role in introducing new ingredients and shaping the style of cuisine in different parts of the country.

Muslims from Turkey, Persia and Afghanistan settled in North India around sixteenth century. The entire country was influenced by the Mughal rule and later by the British. Parsis who migrated to Gujarat around the eight century AD from Iran influenced Gujarati cuisine. Then again, the Portuguese colonized Goa in the early sixteenth century for about 450 years, influencing Goan cuisine. The demand for spices drew traders to the coastal state of Kerala. Thus, in many regions, we witness fusion food in ample measure.

Local cuisines vary significantly, depending on the soil, climate and topography. Locally available spices, herbs, vegetables, fruit, meat and fish characterize the cuisine of a region.

North

NORTH

North India comprises mainly the states of Uttar Pradesh (UP), Uttarakhand, Punjab, Haryana, Himachal Pradesh and the union territories of Delhi and Jammu & Kashmir (now union territory).

JAMMU & KASHMIR

Harsh winters in Kashmir prevent the growth of fresh vegetables and hence there is heavy reliance on dry vegetables and meat. Some exotic vegetarian dishes are Kathal ke Kebab (jackfruit kebab), Kachnar ki Sabzi (flower dish), Bhare Karele (stuffed bitter gourd), Hak (green leafy vegetable), Nadru (lotus stem) and Yakhni (meat in yoghurt gravy).

Jammu is famous for its Rajma. Arhar ki Dal with Shalgam, is another incredibly flavourful dal from Kashmir. A close Kashmiri friend, Rattan Kaul, not only gave me the recipe of the dish, but being an excellent cook himself, also gave me a practical demonstration. I have never ceased to admire this dal ever since.

DELHI

With the incredible diversity of people who make up the national capital, there are many regional and foreign influences. Delhi is regarded as the food capital of the country.

Delhi's love for food is insatiable. Food culture in Delhi is a mix of north Indian food, Mughlai cuisine, Punjabi cuisine and a variety of food from different parts of the country and the world.

Old Delhi is considered to be the street food capital of India. Paranthe Wali Gali in Chandi Chowk offers an incredible variety of paranthas stuffed with aloo, gobhi, mooli and keema. The chaat options are innumerable. Since the Mughals ruled from the capital for centuries, there is a strong Mughal influence to be found in Delhi. Tandoori food is a prominent contribution of that time. There are any number of dhabas, low budget restaurants and five-star hotels offering a variety of cuisines. The variety of food, including dals, whether in dhabas or fancy restaurants is mind boggling. Apart from idli, dosa, sambar and rasam, all lentil-based, we also find Tandoori food and flavourful dals such as Dal Tarka, Rajma, Maa ki Dal, Pindi Chole or Chana Dal, all with different regional flavours
.

PUNJAB

Punjabis are a proud, exuberant, adventurous and fun-loving race. And I must confess I am proud to be one.

In Punjab, dairy products like milk, cream, yoghurt, paneer (cottage cheese) and lassi (butter milk) are used a lot in cooking. Butter and ghee are used liberally. Punjab is home to tandoori roti and naans, tandoori chicken, stuffed paranthas, kulchas and Chole Bhature.

The markets of Amritsar are a great adventure to explore local food. Particularly famous are the Amritsari Wadiyan, papad and the Amritsari Machhi (river fish coated with chickpea and deep fried).

To be found in this section are the famous Dal Makhani and Pindi Chole that go famously well with bhature.

UTTAR PRADESH

The cuisine of UP has a large variety of dishes, both vegetarian and non-vegetarian, to offer. Being a large state, the cuisine of UP shares a lot of its cuisines with the neighbouring states of Delhi, Uttarakhand, Punjab and Haryana. Mughlai and Awadhi (Lucknow) are two famous cuisines of the state. Lucknow is famous for its kebabs—Seekh Kebab, Kakori Kebab, Shami Kebab and even vegetarian kebabs prepared using either Kathal, Arbi, Zimikhand or Rajma.

Included in this section are—Urad Dal, Lucknavi Arhar Dal and Tarka Dal, besides others.

CHANA AUR LAUKI

PREPARATION TIME
10 minutes

COOKING TIME
25 minutes

SERVES
6–8

- 250 g Bengal gram lentils, split and skinned (chana dal)
- ½ tsp turmeric
- 1 tsp ginger, crushed
- ½ tsp cumin seeds
- ½ tsp sonth (dry ginger powder)

  A

- ½ kg green bottle gourd (lauki), cut into large pieces
- Salt

BAGHAR
- 50 ml ghee
- 1 tsp aniseed (saunf)
- 4 cloves
- A pinch of asafoetida (hing)

GARNISH
- A few fresh mint leaves or 1 tsp dried mint leaves

This dal from Kashmir typically uses the more flavoured spices of the region i.e., dry ginger powder, aniseed and asafoetida. These combine wonderfully well with the earthy flavour of Bengal gram lentil (chana dal) and fresh bottle gourd (lauki).

Wash and soak the lentils for 1 hour. Drain the water.

Place the lentils in a heavy-bottom pan. Add all the ingredients at 'A' and salt, along with 2½ glasses of water. Cook on high flame till the dish comes to a boil. Reduce heat, cover the pan with a lid and cook. When the lentils are half done, add the bottle gourd. Cook till the lentils and bottle gourd are tender. As this is a dryish dish, the lentils should absorb all the water with just a hint of moisture remaining.

For the baghar, heat the ghee. Add aniseeds and cloves, and in a few seconds add asafoetida and turn off heat. Add the baghar to the cooked lentils and mix.

Serve hot, garnished with mint.

KASHMIRI ARHAR DAL
WITH SHALGAM

PREPARATION TIME
10 minutes

COOKING TIME
35–40 minutes

SERVES
6–8

The Mughal emperor Jahangir said of Kashmir as, 'Gar firdaus bar uae zamiast, hameeast, hameeast, hameeast' (If there is paradise on earth, it is here, it is here, it is here!)' Kashmir is also known as the fruit bowl of the country, because many fruits are grown there— apples, cherries, peaches, apricot, plums, strawberries, pomegranates and more.

Kashmiris use a number of dry vegetables in their cooking, such as turnips, tomatoes, beans, peas and cabbage, which are dried for use during the harsh winter (when the temperature drops to -10°C). This dish, however, uses fresh turnips (shalgam) with arhar dal, and the result is mind-blowing. One of my favourite dishes.

- 250 g red gram lentils (arhar dal)
- 2 tbsp oil
- 1 tsp cumin seeds
- ½ tsp turmeric powder
- A pinch of asafoetida, soaked in 2 tbsp water
- 2 tsp red chilli powder
- 2–3 green chillies
- 1 tsp garam masala
- Oil for frying
- 5–6 turnips (shalgam), cut into medium-sized pieces
- 2 tsp sugar
- Salt

BAGHAR

- 55 ml oil
- 1 tsp cumin seeds
- 1 onion, sliced
- 20 g ginger, grated

Wash and soak lentils in 3–4 glasses of water for 30 minutes. Drain the water.

Heat the oil in a heavy-base pan. Add cumin seeds and turmeric immediately, followed by asafoetida with the water in which it was soaked and red chilli powder. Add the lentils, salt, green chillies and garam masala, and mix gently. Add 3–4 glasses of water, cover the pan with a lid and cook on high flame and then on medium-low. Cook till the lentils are tender.

When the dal cools slightly, lightly churn the lentils in a blender. Transfer the lentils back to the pan.

Separately heat the oil and lightly fry the turnips. Add the turnips to the lentils along with 2 tsp of sugar. Cook on medium-low flame for about 8–10 minutes.

Heat the oil for the baghar. Add the cumin seeds. When the cumin seeds turn golden brown, add the onion and ginger. When onions turn translucent, add the baghar to the lentils.

Serve hot. Goes well with steamed rice, roti, puri or bread.

MATRA (DRY PEAS)

PREPARATION TIME
15 minutes

COOKING TIME
30–40 minutes

SERVES
6–8

Matra Kulcha is one of the most popular street foods in north India, especially Delhi. One can see a lot of vendors carrying a brass pot full of Matra and bags of kulcha bread all over the city. Tangy and spicy, it is quite a hit with everyone. Though the dish is made using dry peas (matar) it is commonly referred to as Matra.

I learnt to make this dish from my sister, Sunita, who is not only a bright and successful entrepreneur, but also an incredible chef. She often serves Matra with aplomb, as an interesting and delicious addition to any meal.

- 250 g dry pea lentils (sookhey matar)
- 2 tbsp ghee
- 2 tbsp oil
- 2 tsp besan (gram flour)
- 2 tsp cumin powder
- 3 green chillies, chopped
- 1 tsp ginger, chopped
- ¼th tsp kala namak (black salt)
- ½ tsp pepper powder
- 1 tbsp heaped coriander powder
- 1 tsp yellow chilli powder
- 2 tsp chana masala (commercially available)
- 1 tsp amchoor (dry mango powder)
- Salt

X

Wash and soak the matar overnight in 4 glasses of water.

Drain and wash the previously soaked matar and pressure cook with 2–3 glasses of water and salt. Pressure cook till 1 whistle, reduce the flame and cook it further for 5–6 minutes. When the pressure subsides, check whether the matar is tender. If not, add a little water and cook further till tender. Mash lightly.

In a heavy and deep pan, heat ghee and oil. Add gram flour and fry for a minute. Add cumin powder and mix. And then add 1½–2 glasses of water and mix well. Bring to a boil. Then add all the ingredients at 'X'. Cook for 2 minutes and then add the previously boiled matra. Continue cooking for 5–10 minutes on a medium flame. The dish has medium-thick consistency.

Serve hot with sliced onion and chopped green chilli mixed with salt and lime juice, grated radish with salt, red chilli and lime juice, and kulchas.

URAD DAL KHICHRI

PREPARATION TIME
5 minutes

COOKING TIME
15 minutes

SERVES
4–6

- 100 g rice
- 150 g black
  gram lentils, split
  and unskinned
  (urad dal, dali)
- 2 tbsp ghee
- ½ tsp cumin seeds
- 1 tsp whole pepper
- 1 tbsp ginger, crushed
- Salt

The dish is popular in north Indian households. It can be comfort food for some, or even made during festivities. To know how good and flavoursome this khichri is, you just have to try it. So, please go for it.

Wash the lentils and rice, and soak them together in about 3–4 glasses of water for 1 hour. Drain the water, wash them again and set aside.

Heat ghee in a heavy-base pan. Add cumin seeds, pepper and after about 5 seconds, ginger. Transfer the previously soaked lentils and rice to the pan and stir fry for 2–3 minutes. Add salt and 3–4 glasses of water. Cover and cook on a medium flame for about 15–20 minutes. When ready, the rice and lentils should be soft, with sufficient moisture.

Serve hot.

RAJMA (KIDNEY BEANS)

PREPARATION TIME
15 minutes

COOKING TIME
30 minutes

SERVES
6–8

- 300 g red kidney beans (rajma)
- 1 inch cinnamon stick ⎫
- 2 bay leaves ⎬ A
- 5 cloves ⎭
- 66 ml oil
- 3 onions, grated
- 1 tbsp ginger paste
- 1 tbsp garlic paste
- 1½ tsp red chilli powder
- 3 large tomatoes, pureed and sieved
- A few sprigs of fresh green coriander, chopped
- Salt

Rajma is an all-time favourite in almost every home in Northern India. It is consumed with relish not only in homes but is also a proud and popular feature in most dhabas. Rajma is a thick gravy dish made with many Indian whole spices and is generally had in combination with boiled rice.

Wash and soak the rajma in 5 glasses of water over night. Drain the water before cooking.

Pressure cook the rajma in 4–4½ glasses of water and with the spices at 'A' till 2 whistles. Reduce the flame and cook further for 10 minutes. Open the lid when the pressure subsides. The rajma should be tender, with enough water left for cooking further.

Heat oil in a heavy-base pan. Add the onions and fry till golden brown. Add the ginger and garlic paste, and fry for a minute. Add the salt and red chilli powder. Sprinkle a little water from the rajma in the pan to mix the ingredients well. Then add the tomato puree and cook till the tomato is cooked and the oil starts to separate.

Now add the previously boiled rajma and cook on a medium flame for 8 minutes. Add a little water if needed, as the dish has medium consistency. Sprinkle the chopped coriander.

Serve hot with steamed rice.

RAJMA

URAD KI SOOKHI DAL

PREPARATION TIME
10 minutes

COOKING TIME
30 minutes

SERVES
6

Urad dal has many health benefits, being rich in protein, carbohydrates and dietary fibre. It is exceedingly popular for its rich, earthy and delightful flavour, and is extensively used in many culinary preparations, such as dosa, papad and vada.

This dal is a classic Punjabi dish widely used in north India, including Delhi. The seasoning of red chillies and pepper combined with garnish of fresh mint and ginger makes this dish enticingly flavourful.

- 200 g black gram lentils, split and skinned (urad dal, dhuli)
- 2–3 small pieces of ginger, crushed
- Salt

BAGHAR
- 55 ml oil
- 2 onions, sliced
- 2–3 dry red chillies, broken into 2–3 pieces and the seeds removed
- 1 tsp whole black pepper

GARNISH
- A few mint leaves
- 1 tsp ginger, chopped

Wash and soak the lentils in 3 glasses of water for 30 minutes. Drain the water.

Cook the lentils in a heavy-base pan with salt and ginger in 2 glasses of water. Cook first on high flame and then medium flame covered.

To prepare the baghar, heat the oil. Fry the onions till they turn golden brown. Add the red chillies and whole black pepper. When the colour of red chillies darkens, which will be in a few seconds, pour the baghar over the lentils and mix gently.

Serve hot, garnished with mint leaves and chopped ginger.

ARHAR DAL WITH TOMATO CHUTNEY

PREPARATION TIME
10 minutes

COOKING TIME
25 minutes

SERVES
6

- 250 g red gram lentils (arhar dal)
- ⅓rd tsp turmeric powder
- 55 ml oil
- 1 tsp cumin seeds
- 1 onion, chopped
- 1 tbsp ginger chopped
- 2–3 garlic cloves, chopped
- 2 tomatoes, chopped
- A few sprigs of fresh green coriander, chopped
- 2–3 green chillies, each hand broken into 2
- Wedges of 2 limes
- Salt

It is a recipe of fabulous ease and speed. It is incredibly simple yet you will be bowled over. The combination of red gram lentil (arhar dal), with the tomato chutney and the juice of fresh lime is simply tantalizing.

Wash and soak the lentils in 4 glasses of water for 30 minutes. Drain the water.

Pressure cook the lentils in 3–4 glasses of water along with turmeric and salt. After 1 whistle reduce the flame to medium-low flame and cook for another 1–2 minutes. Turn off the flame. When the pressure subsides open the pressure cooker. The lentils at this stage should be tender.

Heat the oil in a heavy-base pan. Add the cumin seeds. When they turn golden brown, add the chopped onion followed by ginger and garlic. After a minute or two, add the chopped tomatoes and fry. After a couple of minutes, add the fresh coriander and green chillies. Immediately add this to the previously boiled lentils and mix.

Bring the lentils to a boil. Serve hot with steaming hot rice and tomato chutney and squeeze the juice of lime over the chutney in the plate.

PINDI CHOLE

PREPARATION TIME
20 minutes

COOKING TIME
45 minutes

SERVES
8

The name of this dish can be traced to Rawalpindi, a city in the Punjab province of Pakistan. A highly popular street food, it is available in most dhabas and restaurants both in Pakistan and India, particularly north India.

Flavoured with several roasted and powdered aromatic spices, it is simply delicious. It is best accompanied by bhatura or lacha parantha and sliced onion sprinkled with salt and red chilli powder. Serve it along with green chillies and wedges of lime.

A family favourite, this dish is ideal for breakfast and lunch, and is a veritable treat.

- 350 g chickpeas (Kabuli chana)
- 1–2 bay leaves
- 1 tsp Assam tea leaves
- 2 tbsp coriander seeds
- 1 tbsp cumin seeds
- 4–5 cloves
- 10–12 peppercorns
- 2 black cardamoms
- 3–4 green cardamom pods
- 1–2 bay leaves
- 1 inch cinnamon stick
- 2 dry whole red chillies
- 2–3 flakes mace
- Oil to fry

A

Wash the chickpeas well. Then, soak them in 5 glasses of water overnight.

Next day, drain the water, wash the chickpeas and pressure cook in 4 glasses of water along with salt and bay leaves. Cook till 3–4 whistles on a high flame.

Lower the heat and cook over a slow flame for about 5–7 minutes. Turn off the heat. When the pressure subsides, remove the lid. The chickpeas should be tender and there should be about 1 glass of water left in the chickpeas when cooked.

Rinse a tea pot with hot water. Put the tea leaves in. Add 1 cup of boiling water and let the tea brew for 1–2 minutes. Then strain and add the tea to the chickpeas. This will give a rich brown colour to the dish.

Dry roast all the spices mentioned at 'A' to a rich brown colour. Cool a little and grind to a fine powder.

Continued...

- 2 medium potatoes,
  cut into cubes
- 3 tbsp oil
- 2 tomatoes, each cut
  into 4 pieces
- Salt

GARNISH
- 1 tomato, sliced round
- 1 tsp ginger julienne
- 1 medium onion,
  sliced round
- Wedges of 1 lemon

Heat the oil and fry the cubed potatoes till they are golden and cooked. Set aside.

Heat the oil. Add the tomatoes and after 2 minutes add the powdered spices and mix. Take about ½ a glass of water from the chickpeas, add to the spices and mix. Return the ingredients to the chickpeas and mix. Also add the fried potatoes.

Cook for 5 minutes. The dish has a thickish consistency.

Serve hot, garnished with tomatoes and ginger julienne in the center. Decorate the sides of the dish with onions and wedges of lemon.

Goes well with puri, bhatura and lacha parantha.

BHATURE

PREPARATION TIME
15 minutes

COOKING TIME
20 minutes

SERVES
4–6

- 400 g maida (refined flour)
- 3 tbsp suji (semolina)
- 250 g yoghurt   } A
- ½ tsp baking powder
- 1½ tbsp oil
- Oil to fry
- ¼th tsp salt

Next time you think of breaking bread, think of bhature. Soft and delicate to the touch and taste, bhatures and Pindi Chole make perfect combination. They are hugely popular not only in Punjab but also the adjoining north Indian states.

. . . .

Mix all ingredients at 'A', along with salt and knead for about 10–12 minutes to make a soft dough. Sprinkle a little water while kneading, as may be required.

Once the dough is well kneaded, cover and keep it in the fridge overnight or covered at room temperature for at least 1–2 hours before making bhature.

Now divide the dough equally into 10 portions. Take each portion in your palm and roll it with both hands into a round ball. Apply a little oil on the ball and using a roller pin, roll each ball into an oval shape bhatura about 4–5 inches in length.

Heat the oil in a deep and wide pan (preferably a kadhai) for frying. Immerse one bhatura at a time and fry till light golden.

Serve hot.

A rather nice accompaniment would be sliced onion, sliced green chillies together with sliced fresh lime to provide added zest to this most delicious combination of bhature and Pindi Chole.

PINDI CHOLE AND BHATURE

DAL MAKHANI

PREPARATION TIME
10 minutes

COOKING TIME
50 minutes

SERVES
8–10

- 200 g black gram lentils, whole (urad dal, sabut)
- 50 g red kidney beans (rajma)
- 1 black cardamom ⎫
- 1 inch cinnamon stick
- 2–3 cloves
- 5–6 peppercorns   ⎬ A
- 2 dry whole red chillies
- 2 bay leaves ⎭
- 66 ml oil
- 1 onion, chopped
- 1 tsp ginger paste
- 1 tsp garlic paste
- 1 tsp red chilli powder
- 4 tomatoes, pureed and sieved
- 100 g fresh cream
- 50 g butter
- 1 tsp ginger julienne
- Salt

It is one of the most popular dals that originated from Punjab. Buttery soft, creamy and delicious, you will find it being sold both in dhabas as well as in five-star hotels. It is a favourite dish for a regular meal or a party, normally served with hot naans and onions soaked in vinegar.

Wash the lentils (urad and rajma) well and soak in 5 glasses of water overnight.

The next day, drain and wash the lentils. Pressure cook the lentils in 4 glasses of water along with all the ingredients mentioned at 'A' and salt. Pressure cook till 3–4 whistles and then cook for on a low flame for about 10–15 minutes. Turn off the heat. When the pressure subsides, uncover. The lentils should be tender and golden brown in colour. If necessary, cook further, partly covered, on low flame for another 5–10 minutes.

Heat oil in a separate pan. Add the onions and fry till they turn golden. Add the ginger and garlic paste. In a few seconds add the red chilli powder, followed by tomato puree. When the tomato puree is cooked a little and the oil starts to separate, add it to the cooked lentils and mix. Cook further for 10 minutes on a low flame.

Add fresh cream, reserving a little for garnish. Also, add butter.

Serve hot, garnished with fresh cream and julienned ginger.

Goes well with tandoori roti, naan or parantha.

DAL GOSHT

PREPARATION TIME
10 minutes

COOKING TIME
30 minutes

SERVES
6–8

If you are looking for a gourmet experience, try this dish. A rich and delicious mingling of flavours—lentil, meat and whole and ground spices with juice of lime makes it ever so seductive in flavour. The garnish adds colour to the dish and makes it both flavourful and visually appealing.

- 200 g red lentils, split and skinned (masoor dal, dhuli)
- ¼th tsp turmeric powder
- 65 ml oil
- 4 onions, cut in the middle horizontally and then sliced fine
- 1 inch cinnamon stick
- 5 cloves
- 7–8 whole pepper
- 1 bay leaf
- 1 kg meat, cut into medium-sized pieces
- 1 tsp ginger paste
- 1 tsp garlic paste
- 2 tsp coriander powder
- 1 tsp meat masala (a good brand, commercially available)
- ⅓rd tsp turmeric powder
- 1½ tsp red chilli powder
- Juice of 1½ lime
- Salt

BAGHAR
- 2 tbsp oil
- 1 onion, cut horizontally and then sliced fine
- 2–3 dry red chillies
- ½ tsp red chilli powder

Wash and soak the lentils in 4 glasses of water for 30 minutes. Drain the water. Place the lentils in a heavy-base pan. Add 2½ glasses of water along with turmeric and salt.

Cook first on high flame for 4–5 minutes and then reduce flame and cook partly covered. Cook till the lentils are tender.

Heat the oil in a pressure cooker. Add the onions and fry. Also add the whole spices i.e., cinnamon, cloves, whole pepper and bay leaf. When the onions turn golden, add the meat and the salt. Fry for about 10 minutes till the water in the meat dries up. Then add the ginger and garlic paste and fry for 1–2 minutes. Now add the coriander powder, meat masala, turmeric powder and red chilli powder. Fry for 1–2 minutes and then add 3 glasses of water. Pressure cook till 2 whistles and then reduce flame and cook further for 10 minutes.

Open the lid of the pressure cooker when the pressure subsides. Squeeze the juice of lime. Add the previously boiled lentils. Mix and cook for 5–6 minutes. This dish has medium-thick consistency so, if necessary, add a little water while cooking the meat and lentils together.

For baghar, heat the oil in a separate pan. Add the dry red chillies and then in a few seconds the onion. When the onion turns golden, turn off the flame and add the red chilli powder.

Serve hot, garnished with the above baghar and steaming hot rice.

ARHAR DAL FLAVOURED WITH GARLIC

PREPARATION TIME
20 minutes

COOKING TIME
30 minutes

SERVES
6–8

- 250 g red gram lentils (arhar dal)
- 1/3rd tsp turmeric powder
- 1 tsp yellow chilli powder
- 1 tsp ginger paste
- 1 tsp garlic paste
- 1 tbsp white butter, unsalted
- Salt

BAGHAR

- 2 tbsp white butter, unsalted
- 10–12 garlic cloves, crushed
- 1 tsp cumin seeds
- 4–5 dry red chillies

A simple and flavourful dal from UP, enriched with white unsalted butter and the star of the dish—garlic.

Wash and soak the lentils in water, 3 inches above the surface of the lentils. Soak for 30 minutes. Drain just before cooking.

Take a heavy-bottomed pan. Place the drained lentils in it. Add salt, yellow chilli powder, ginger paste and garlic paste. Add 3 glasses of water. Cook covered, first on a high flame till the dish comes to a boil and then on low. Cook covered till the lentils are tender. Add butter and stir.

For the baghar, heat the butter. Add crushed garlic, followed in 15–20 seconds by the cumin seeds. A few seconds later, add the red chillies. When the chillies turn reddish-brown, add the baghar to the lentils.

This dal has medium-thick consistency. Serve hot.

MOONG KI BIKHARI DAL

PREPARATION TIME
5–10 minutes

COOKING TIME
20 minutes

SERVES
6

- 200 g green gram lentils, split and skinned (moong dal, dhuli)
- 55 ml oil
- 1 tsp cumin seeds
- 1 tsp peppercorns
- 1 large onion, chopped
- 2–3 green chillies, chopped
- 15–20 curry leaves
- 1 tsp freshly crushed pepper
- Salt

This is a simple but delicious dal with a beautiful name. The name suggests scattered lentils, where though tender each grain is still separate. I owe this recipe to Nikhat Mahdi. It is one of my favourite dals.

Wash and soak the lentils for 1 hour. Drain the water.

Heat the oil. Add cumin seeds, followed by peppercorns. Add onion and fry for a few seconds and then add the green chillies. When the onion turns translucent, add curry leaves.

Add the drained lentils and salt, and 1½ glasses of water. Cook covered on high flame till the dish comes to a boil. Then reduce flame to medium-low and cook covered till the lentils are tender. Sprinkle a little water, if necessary.

When done, each grain should be tender yet separate with just a hint of moisture. Turn off the heat and add crushed pepper and mix gently.

Serve hot.

SOOKHI MOONG DAL

PREPARATION TIME
15 minutes

COOKING TIME
20 minutes

SERVES
6

- 200 g green gram lentils, split and skinned (moong dal, dhuli)
- 50 g ghee
- 8 dry red chillies
- 3 onions, finely sliced
- 1 tsp caraway seeds
- 4–5 green cardamom pods
- 2 tbsp coriander seeds, lightly crushed
- 1 tsp ginger paste
- Salt

Moong dal is a light and flavourful dal. It is easy on the stomach and is, therefore, given even to babies as their first food.

Delicately spiced, the beauty of this dal is evident when served from the pan to a serving dish in its original formation.

Wash and soak the lentils in 4 glasses of water for 1 hour. Drain the water.

Heat the ghee in a heavy-base pan with a tight-fitting lid. Add the red chillies. When the colour of chillies becomes red-brown, remove the chillies from the pan and set aside. Keep the pan on low heat.

Now, except salt, mix all the remaining ingredients, including the red chillies, with the sliced onions. Place the mixture evenly over the ghee left in the pan. Next spread the lentils over this onion mixture. Add salt to 1 glass of water and sprinkle evenly over the lentils. Cover with a tight fitting lid. If necessary, put a heavy stone on the lid to prevent the steam from escaping. Cook on high flame till the pan gets hot. Then reduce heat and cook for about 15–20 minutes till the lentils are tender. If need be, sprinkle a little water and cook further till the lentils become tender.

Carefully lift the lentils with the help of a large slotted ladle and place them in a serving dish so that the original formation is not disturbed i.e., the onion mixture should form the base and lentils should be placed over them. Serve hot.

TARKA DAL

PREPARATION TIME
10 minutes

COOKING TIME
25–30 minutes

SERVES
4–5

A great dish where butter adds a rich and deep flavour, while ginger and caraway seeds add piquancy.

- 50 g black gram lentils, split and skinned (urad dal, dhuli)
- 50 g Bengal gram lentils, split and skinned (chana dal)
- 50 g green gram lentils, split and skinned (moong dal, dhuli)
- 50 g red lentils, split and skinned (masoor dal, dhuli)
- ½ tsp turmeric powder
- 1 tsp red chilli powder
- A small piece of ginger, crushed
- ½ tsp garam masala
- Salt

BAGHAR

- 3 tsp unsalted butter
- 1 tsp oil
- 1 tsp caraway seeds (shah jeera)
- 1 medium onion, chopped
- A small piece of ginger, chopped
- 5–6 garlic cloves, chopped

GARNISH

- A few sprigs of fresh green coriander, chopped

Wash and soak the lentils in water for 20 minutes. Drain the water.

Place the lentils in a heavy-bottom pan along with salt, turmeric, red chilli powder and ginger. Add 2½ glasses of water and cook first on a high flame and then a medium-low flame, partially covered till the lentils are tender. Add garam masala and mix. Add a little hot water, if required, as this dal has medium-thick consistency.

For the baghar, heat butter and oil. Add caraway seeds. When they turn slightly brown, add the onions, followed by ginger and garlic. When the onions turn golden brown, add the baghar to the lentils and mix.

Serve hot, garnished with fresh green coriander.

South

SOUTH

South Indian states primarily comprise Andhra Pradesh, Telangana, Tamil Nadu, Karnataka and Kerala.

ANDHRA PRADESH AND TELANGANA

Hyderabad is a very plural city. It is a synthesis of many cultures living in harmony. Mughals, Persians and Arab have all influenced the Hyderabadi cuisine. But it is the Telugu cuisine that has contributed most to the tang and perkiness of Hyderabadi food. It is generally hot and spicy, with liberal use of chillies and tamarind. The array of pulaos, biryanis, kababs and kormas are the pride of Hyderabadi cuisine.

Hyderabadi vegetarian dishes have a sparkling and lively quality. The dals in Hyderabad come in several varieties. Meethi Dal, Khatti Dal, Dalcha with vegetables and meat. One of the hot favourite dals of Hyderabad is Khatti Dal. When people have this dal, all they want is more. Another quick and reassuringly undemanding dal from Hyderabad is Lassan aur Lal Mirch ki Arhar ki Dal, which I learnt from family friend Ghulam Haider. Thikri ki Dal is not only exquisite in flavour but looks highly exotic too. You can serve this dal triumphantly at parties. Another gustily flavoured dal is Mutton ka Dalcha with Drumsticks —just the dish to bowl you over.

TAMIL NADU

Tamil Nadu, as also other southern states, are known for the wide range of spices such as chillies, tamarind, cloves, cardamom, pepper and coriander. Coconut, coconut oil, curry leaves and drumsticks are used in abundance.

South Indian food has earned much fame not only in southern states, but, across the globe. Masala dosa can be found across the world. Some other equally popular dishes include idli, sambar, vada and uttapam. Tamil Nadu also offers many other flavourful dishes such as curd rice, upma, lemon rice, payasam and many biryani and mutton dishes. Snacks such as banana chips and bondas are hugely popular.

Some amazing dals and lentil-based dishes such as Kootu, Mixed Dal Rasam, Arhar Dal with Vegetables and Payasam (moong dal with jaggery, flavoured with cardamom and saffron) find place in this section.

KARNATAKA

The traditional cuisine of Karnataka is known for its generous use of jaggery, palm sugar and limited use of chilli powder.

Karnataka is the mildest in terms of spice content among the five South Indian states. North Karnataka cuisine, however, is an exception and can be highly fiery and spicy. Coorg is known for its wide use of pork, meat and game. Kokum is generously used.

Coastal Karnataka makes wide-spread use of sea food, coconut and coconut oil.

Lentils and vegetables are cooked with coconut, spices and tempered with mustard, curry leaves and asafoetida.

Karnataka offers a wide range of appetizing dishes. Masala dosa, idli and vada are said to have originated in the temple streets of the city of Udupi.

Bisi Bele Huliyana is a famous and traditional dish of Karnataka. An unbelievable medley of lentils, rice and a host of vegetables, this dish finds place in the following section.

KERALA

Situated on the south-west coast of India with its lush, tropical land and tranquil backwaters, Kerala abounds in spices. Coconut, fish and prawn are available in plenty as also curry leaves, shallots and green chillies. Vegetables such as tapioca, yam, colocasia, pumpkin, drumsticks and banana flowers are all staples of Kerala cuisine.

Demand for pepper and other spices such as cloves, cardamom, cinnamon, and nutmeg drew traders from Arabia, Egypt, Greece, Italy and China to this land. The Portuguese, Dutch, French and English all vied with each other to capture and hold the lucrative spice trade. Many settled in Kerala. Thus, we find many Muslims, Jews and Christians living in the state. They also strongly influenced the local cuisine. Syrian Christian and Malabari Muslim dishes are now becoming popular across the country. Malayali cuisine is characterized by its imaginative and delicate use of spices, despite their availability in plenty.

During one of our visits to Kerala, we stayed in Kumarakom Lake Resort—a popular tourist destination and famous for its lovely backwaters. While cruising on the backwaters, we came across a two-roomed hut on the bank with a beckoning sign that read 'Hawaii'. A garden umbrella was perched in front, with a coarse wooden table and four chairs. Our curiosity aroused, we sat ourselves down at the place. There was a husband-and-wife team

ready to cook jumbo prawns for us, which they did right in front of us. My family gorged on the delicious prawns that the couple cooked and served.

Popular Kerala dishes include sambar, rasam, stews—vegetarian and non-vegetarian— served with appam, shrimp and fish curries. Kerala also offers a dazzling array of biryanis.

Included in the section that follows are some truly flavourful lentil-based dishes such as a spice flavoured Kerala Dal, Masoor Dal and Bitter Gourd Theeyal, Payar Thenga, Muringakai Theeyal and more.

TELANGANA SAMBAR

PREPARATION TIME
20 minutes

COOKING TIME
45 minutes

SERVES
8

- 250 g mix of red gram lentils (arhar dal), Bengal gram lentils, split and skinned (chana dal), ochre lentils (masoor dal, sabut) and green gram lentils, split and skinned (moong dal, dhuli)
- ⅓rd tsp turmeric powder
- 55 ml oil
- 1 tsp mustard seeds
- 1 tsp cumin
- ½ tsp caraway seeds
- 1–2 bay leaves
- 3–4 cloves
- 1 tsp ginger paste
- 1 tsp garlic paste
- 2 tomatoes, chopped into medium-sized pieces
- green gourd
- radish
- okra
- drum stick
- pumpkin
- onion

  } cut into medium-sized pieces so that the combined chopped weight is about 300 g

- 2 tsp red chilli powder
- 2 green chillies, slit down the middle
- 15–20 curry leaves
- 50 g tamarind, soaked in warm water for 10 minutes, mashed and strained
- 2 tbsp jaggery
- A few sprigs of fresh green coriander, chopped
- Salt

Generally, the hot and spicy Telangana cuisine has a sparkling and lively quality. Lentils cooked with a medley of vegetables, soured with tamarind and tempered with spices, make this a tantalizing Telangana experience.

. . . .

Wash and soak the lentils for 20 minutes. Drain the water.

Pressure cook the lentils in 3–4 glasses of water, a little salt and turmeric. After 1 whistle, reduce the flame to medium-low and cook for another 3–4 minutes. Turn off the flame. When the pressure subsides, open the pressure cooker. The lentils at this stage should be tender. Mash lightly.

Heat the oil in a heavy-bottom pan. Add the mustard seeds. When they start to splutter, add cumin seeds, caraway seeds, bay leaves, cloves and then the ginger and garlic paste. After 15–20 seconds, add the tomatoes and the vegetables. Stir fry for 5 minutes.

Now add the lentils, red chilli powder, green chillies, curry leaves, tamarind and jaggery. Mix and cook partly covered for about 7–8 minutes till the vegetables are tender. Finally sprinkle fresh green coriander.

The dish has medium consistency.

Serve hot. Goes well with hot steamed rice.

TELANGANA SAMBAR

LASSAN AUR LAL MIRCH KI ARHAR KI DAL

PREPARATION TIME
15 minutes

COOKING TIME
30 minutes

SERVES
6

- 200 g red gram lentils (arhar dal)
- 1 pod garlic, peeled
- 8 dry red chillies
- Salt

BAGHAR
- 65 ml ghee
- 6–7 dry red chillies, broken

This dish glamorises the ordinary. Incredibly simple to make, the chillies give this dish a high and ghee infuses it with awesome flavour.

. . . .

Wash and soak the lentils in 3–4 glasses of water for 30 minutes. Drain the water.

Grind the garlic into a fine paste. Then add the red chillies, a little salt and grind further, coarsely.

Place the lentils in a heavy-base pan. Add 3 glasses of water and cook first on a high flame till it comes to a boil and then on a medium-low flame. Cook till tender. Mash lightly.

Add the garlic and chilli paste, and salt to the lentils. Also add a little water, if required. The dish has medium-thick consistency. Cook on a medium-low flame for about 10 minutes.

Heat the ghee. Break the chillies and separate the seeds. Lower the flame before adding both the chillies and seeds to the ghee. When the chillies turn red-brown, pour the baghar over the lentils and mix.

Serve hot.

KADDU KA DALCHA

PREPARATION TIME
20 minutes

COOKING TIME
30 minutes

SERVES
6–8

A very Hyderabadi dish, and a family favourite. It combines the earthy flavours of lentils with the freshness of the green bottle gourd. A simple recipe but a winner too.

. . . .

- 200 g lentils (arhar, masoor or chana dal), individually or in combination
- ⅓rd tsp turmeric powder
- 1 tsp red chilli powder
- 50 ml tamarind
- 2 tomatoes, chopped
- 55 ml oil
- ½ tsp mustard seeds
- 1 tsp cumin seeds
- 2 medium onions, sliced
- 1 tsp ginger and garlic paste
- 15–20 curry leaves
- 500 g green bottle gourd (kaddu or ghia), peeled and cut into 2 x ¾th-inch pieces
- ½ tsp cumin powder
- Salt

Wash the lentils and soak in 3½ glasses of water for 20 minutes.

Wash and soak tamarind in one cup warm water for 10–15 minutes. Mash and sieve to get tamarind juice.

Add salt, turmeric and red chilli powder to the lentils, using the same water in which they were soaked. Cook in a heavy-base pan covered with a lid, first on high flame and then medium-low flame. Cook till almost tender. Mash a little. Add tamarind juice and tomatoes and cook for about 10 minutes.

Heat the oil. Add mustard seeds, followed by cumin seeds. When the mustard seeds start to splutter and the cumin seeds turn golden brown, add the sliced onions. When the onions turn golden brown, add the ginger and garlic paste, and curry leaves. In a few seconds, add the green bottle gourd, mix, cover and cook on a medium-low flame till almost tender.

Add the green gourd to the lentils. Also add the cumin powder. Cook for 2–3 minutes on low flame.

Dalcha should have medium consistency. Accordingly the water can be adjusted while cooking.

Serve hot with plain rice, puri or roti.

MASOOR KI KHATTI DAL

PREPARATION TIME
20 minutes

COOKING TIME
30 minutes

SERVES
6–8

- 200 g red lentils
  (masoor dal, dhuli)
- ¼th tsp turmeric
  powder
- 1 tsp red chilli powder
- 100 g cauliflower
- 2 carrots
- 3–4 small brinjals
- 1 radish
- 100 g French beans

BAGHAR
- 55 ml oil
- ½ tsp mustard seeds
- 8–10 cloves of garlic,
  crushed
- A few curry leaves
- 2 medium onions,
  sliced
- 2 tomatoes, chopped
- Juice of 2 limes
- Salt

A simple and easy dish to prepare, where the flavour of lentils, combined with a host of fresh vegetables is enhanced by nice tempering of fresh lime juice.

. . . .

Wash the lentils well and soak in 3 glasses of water for 20 minutes before draining them.

Take a heavy-base pan. Cook the lentils along with salt, turmeric and red chilli powder in 3 glasses of water. Cook first on a high flame and then medium-low flame till they are 60 per cent done.

Add all the vegetables cut into 1½-inch pieces. Cook till the vegetables are just tender. Make sure they are not too soft.

Heat the oil and add mustard seeds. When they start to splutter, add crushed garlic. When the garlic turns golden, add curry leaves, followed by onions. When the onions turn golden brown, add chopped tomatoes. Cook for 2–3 minutes till the tomatoes turn soft. Then add the baghar to the lentils and pour the lime juice over it.

Serve hot. Goes well with steamed rice.

MASOOR KI
KHATTI DAL

CHANE KI DAL TAMATER AUR METHI KE SAATH

PREPARATION TIME
20 minutes

COOKING TIME
30 minutes

SERVES
8–10

- 200 g Bengal gram lentils, split and skinned (chana dal)
- 82 ml oil
- 2 onions, chopped
- 2 green chillies, broken by hand
- ½ tsp ginger paste
- ½ tsp garlic paste
- ⅓rd tsp turmeric powder
- 1 tsp red chilli powder
- 500 g tomatoes, skin peeled and chopped
- 1 cup freshly plucked fenugreek leaves, coarsely chopped
- Salt

This is a dish from Hyderabad and made often at our home, especially during winter when fresh fenugreek is available in plenty.

The earthy richness of chana dal combines beautifully with the sour and tangy flavour of tomatoes, and the sweet and nutty flavour of fenugreek.

. . . .

Wash and soak the lentils in water for 1 hour. Drain the water.

Pressure cook the lentils in about 2 glasses of water till 1–2 whistles. Lower the flame and cook further for 1–2 minutes. Turn off the flame and open the lid once the steam subsides. The lentils should be just about tender, and not overcooked.

Heat the oil. Add the onions, followed in just about a minute by the green chillies. When the onions turn golden brown, add ginger and garlic paste. After a few seconds, add salt, turmeric and red chilli powder. Mix and fry a little, and then add the tomatoes. Cook for about 7–8 minutes.

Add the fresh fenugreek. Cook for 5–6 minutes and then mix in the previously boiled chana dal. Cover and cook for about another 5 minutes.

The dish should have medium-thick consistency.

Serve hot.

KULFE KA DALCHA

PREPARATION TIME
20 minutes

COOKING TIME
30 minutes

SERVES
6

Kulfa, known in English as 'purslane', with reddish stems and dark green leaves, is a succulent plant with a mildly sour and unique flavour. It combines beautifully with split gram lentils in this dish. Cooked in the manner described in this recipe, it translates into an unbelievably delicious dish. In Hyderabad, kulfa is also cooked with mutton and is greatly relished.

- 250 g Bengal gram lentils, split and skinned (chana dal)
- ½ tsp turmeric
- 66 ml oil
- 300 g purslane (kulfa), leaves picked and washed
- 2 onions, sliced
- ¾th tsp ginger paste
- ¾th tsp garlic paste
- 3–4 green chillies, each broken into 2 by hand
- Salt

BAGHAR
- 3 tbsp ghee
- ½ tsp mustard seeds
- ½ tsp cumin seeds
- 5–6 cloves of garlic, crushed
- 6 dry whole red chillies
- A few curry leaves

Soak the lentils in 3–4 glasses of water for 30 minutes. Drain the water and wash the lentils again.

Place the lentils in a pressure cooker. Add 2½ glasses of water, salt and turmeric. Pressure cook till 2–3 whistles, lower the heat and cook for another 6–7 minutes. Open the cooker once the pressure subsides. The lentils should be tender with a little water left in the cooker.

Heat 2 tbsp oil. Add the kulfa with a little salt and turmeric. Cook till almost tender. Set aside.

In a heavy-base pan, heat the remaining oil. Add the onions and fry till golden-brown. Add ginger and garlic, and fry for a minute. Add the lentils and the Kulfa. Add a little water and bring to a boil. Add green chillies and cook for 5–6 minutes till the dish blends.

To make the baghar, heat the ghee. Add mustard seeds, followed by cumin seeds. When the mustard seeds start to crackle, add garlic, followed in a few seconds by dry whole red chillies. Next, add the curry leaves. When the chillies darken, pour the baghar over the lentils and mix.

The dish has medium consistency. Serve hot. Goes well with steaming hot plain rice.

MUTTON DALCHA WITH DRUMSTICKS

PREPARATION TIME
20 minutes

COOKING TIME
45 minutes

SERVES
6

Delicious and rich, this is a typically Hyderabadi recipe where the lentils are combined with mutton, marrow bones and tender ribs of a goat and finally cooked with lightly fried drumsticks. The flavour of this dish is given an exciting lift with a blend of spices, chillies—both red and green—and tamarind. Usually served with steaming hot plain rice, this is also my son Gaurav's favourite dish.

Drumstick trees are easy to grow. Not only are drumsticks flavourful, they offer a plethora of health benefits. They are good for diabetes and digestion. They strengthen bones. They also purify blood, help in respiratory disorders and more. A drumstick tree in full bloom is a visual treat and looks like a beautiful Chinese painting, what with its ever-so-pale green and exquisitely delicate flowers and drumsticks hanging in profusion. I have never been able to resist the temptation of planting drumstick trees in my garden wherever I was posted.

- 250 g lentils, a mix of 100 g red lentils (masoor dal), 100 g red gram lentils (arhar dal) and 50 g Bengal gram lentils, split and skinned (chana dal)
- ½ tsp turmeric
- 110 ml oil
- 5–6 drumsticks cut into 3-inch-sized pieces
- ½ tsp caraway seeds
- ½ inch cinnamon stick
- 4 cloves

Wash and soak the lentils in 4 glasses of water for 20 minutes. Drain the water.

Pressure cook the lentils in 3 glasses of water with a little salt and ¼th tsp of turmeric, till 1–2 whistles. Turn off the flame and open the pressure cooker once the steam subsides.

Simultaneously heat the oil in a pressure cooker. Lightly fry the drumsticks and set aside.

To the same oil, add the caraway seeds, cinnamon, cloves and cardamom, followed by the onions. Fry till the onions are golden brown. Then add ginger and garlic paste. Fry for just about a minute. Add the

Continued...

- 2 green cardamom pods
- 2 medium onions, finely sliced
- ½ tsp ginger paste
- ½ tsp garlic paste
- ¼th tsp turmeric powder
- 1 tsp red chilli powder
- 1½ tbsp musk melon and watermelon seeds, ground
- 600 g mutton (marrow bones with some meat on them and tender ribs of goat)
- 75 g tamarind (soaked in warm water for 15 minutes, washed and sieved)
- 2–3 green chillies, hand broken
- A few sprigs of coriander, chopped.
- Salt

BAGHAR
- 2 tbsp oil
- 1 tsp mustard seeds
- 1 tsp sesame seeds
- 1 tbsp shallots, sliced fine
- A few curry leaves

balance of turmeric, red chilli and a little salt and the ground musk and water melon seeds. Fry just a little. Sprinkle a little water and mix well.

Add the meat and fry till the water dries up. Add 2½ glasses of water to the meat and pressure cook till 2–3 whistles. Reduce the flame and cook further for 8–10 minutes till the meat is tender.

When the meat is tender, add the boiled lentils and drumsticks. Wait for 5 minutes before adding the tamarind juice, green chillies and coriander, and cook further for 5 minutes.

For the baghar, heat the ghee. Add all the baghar ingredients, fenugreek seeds last of all. When the red chillies darken, add the baghar to the Dalcha and cover immediately to capture the aroma.

MOONGE KI PHALLI KI KHATTI DAL

PREPARATION TIME
20 minutes

COOKING TIME
30 minutes

SERVES
6

- 200 g red gram lentils (arhar dal)
- ⅓rd tsp turmeric powder
- 82 ml oil
- 8–10 drumsticks, cut into 2–3-inch pieces
- 1 small onion, sliced
- 2–3 green chillies chopped
- 2 tomatoes, blanched, skin removed and coarsely chopped
- 1 tsp red chilli powder
- 15–20 curry leaves
- 50 g tamarind, washed and soaked in 1 glass warm water for 10 minutes and strained to get tamarind juice.
- Salt

BAGHAR
- 2 tbsp oil
- 1 tsp cumin seeds
- 8–10 garlic cloves, crushed
- 7–8 dry red chillies
- 15–20 curry leaves

The amazing and highly nutritious drumsticks are called 'Moonge ki Phalli' in Hyderabad. There is a rich and delicious intermingling of flavours that makes this dish a true delight. This dish is also often made with mutton.

Wash and soak the lentils for about 20 minutes. Drain the water. Add a little salt and turmeric, and 3 glasses of water to the lentils and cook till tender.

In a separate pan, heat the oil. Add the drumsticks and fry lightly. Remove the drumsticks and set aside.

In the same oil, fry the onion till golden. Add the green chillies, followed by tomatoes. After 3–4 minutes, add this to the lentils. Also add red chilli powder, curry leaves, tamarind juice and the previously-fried drumsticks. Mix and cook partly covered on a medium flame for about 5–7 minutes.

Heat the oil. Add cumin seeds. When they turn brown, add garlic and after about 10–15 seconds, add the whole red chillies, followed by curry leaves.

Heat the lentils and transfer to a serving dish. Pour the baghar over the dish as garnish.

MIXED KHATTI DAL

PREPARATION TIME
10–15 minutes

COOKING TIME
20 minutes

SERVES
6–8

It is a quintessential Hyderabadi dish made with a mix of three dals and an extravagant blend of spices. The flavour of this dal is sharpened with lots of lemon juice.

- 150 g red gram lentils (arhar dal)
- 75 g red lentils (masoor dal, dhuli)
- 75 g green gram lentils, split and skinned (moong dal, dhuli)
- ⅓rd tsp turmeric powder
- 55 ml oil + 1 tsp oil
- ½ tsp cumin seeds ⎫
- 2 green cardamom pods ⎪
- 1 black cardamom pod ⎪
- ½ tsp peppercorns ⎬ A
- 2–3 cloves ⎪
- 1 bay leaf ⎪
- 2–3 dry whole red chillies ⎭
- 1 onion, sliced
- 1 tsp ginger and garlic paste
- A few curry leaves
- 2 tomatoes, chopped
- ½ tsp cumin powder ⎫
- ½ tsp coriander powder ⎪
- 1 tsp red chilli powder ⎬ B
- A pinch of garam masala ⎭
- Juice of 2 limes
- Salt

Wash and soak all three lentils in 5 glasses of water for 30 minutes. Drain the lentils.

In a heavy-base pan, boil the lentils in about 3 glasses of water along with turmeric powder and 1 tsp oil. Boil without a lid and cook only till it is about 50 per cent done.

Heat the oil in a heavy-base pan. Add all the ingredients at 'A'. After about 5–10 seconds, add the sliced onion.

When the onions turn translucent, add ginger and garlic paste, and the curry leaves. Fry a little till the onions are golden brown. Add tomatoes and fry a little. Then add all the powdered spices at 'B'. Mix it well.

Now add the previously boiled lentils and mix. Cook covered for about 10–12 minutes till the lentils are tender. Turn off the flame and add the lime juice.

This dal has medium-thick consistency.

Serve hot.

MOONG AUR PALAK

PREPARATION TIME
20 minutes

COOKING TIME
30 minutes

SERVES
6–8

- 250 g green gram
  lentils, split and
  skinned (moong dal,
  dhuli)
- ¼th tsp turmeric
  powder
- 55 ml oil
- ½ tsp ginger paste
- ½ tsp garlic paste
- 300 g fresh green
  spinach, picked,
  washed and chopped
- 2–3 green chillies,
  each hand-broken
  into 2
- Salt

BAGHAR
- 4 tbsp ghee
- ½ tsp cumin seeds
- 5–6 cloves of garlic,
  crushed
- 4–5 dry whole red
  chillies
- A few curry leaves

Green gram lentils (split and skinned) and fresh green spinach, are both highly nutritious and work beautifully together in this dish. Incorporating aromatic spices and ghee, this dish acquires an amazing flavour.

Wash and soak the lentils in 3 glasses of water for 20 minutes.

Boil the lentils in 3 glasses of water with salt and turmeric, without pressure, till tender. Keep aside.

Heat the oil, add ginger and garlic, and after a minute, the spinach. Cook till almost tender.

Next mix the cooked spinach with lentils. Add the green chillies and a little water if necessary. Cook for about 5 minutes.

For baghar, heat the ghee. Add the cumin seeds, garlic, dry whole red chillies and curry leaves. When the red chillies darken, pour the baghar over the lentils and cover. This dish has medium-thick consistency.

Serve hot.

CHANA DAL WITH KEEMA AND FRESH FENUGREEK

PREPARATION TIME
25 minutes

COOKING TIME
40 minutes

SERVES
6–8

- 150 g Bengal gram lentils, split and skinned (chana dal)
- ⅓rd cup oil
- ½ tsp fenugreek seeds (methi)
- 2 onions, finely sliced
- 2–3 green chillies, chopped
- 1 tsp ginger paste
- 1 tsp garlic paste
- ⅓rd tsp turmeric powder
- 1 tsp red chilli powder
- A few sprigs of fresh green coriander, chopped
- A few mint leaves, coarsely chopped
- 250 g keema (minced meat)
- 1 cup fresh fenugreek leaves (methi saag), coarsely chopped
- Juice of 1–2 limes
- Salt

Rich and invigorating in taste with its finely balanced combination of flavours, this is a delicious dish from Hyderabad. It is sharpened with lemon juice, this dish is not unexpectedly seductive.

Wash and soak the lentils for about 20 minutes. Drain the water.

Place the lentils in a heavy-base pan and add about 2–3 glasses of water and a little salt (just enough for the lentils to cook while covered) first on a high flame till the lentils come to a boil and then on medium-low flame till the lentils are tender. Set it aside.

Heat the oil in a separate heavy-base pan. Add fenugreek seeds, followed by onions and the green chillies. When the onions turn golden, add ginger and garlic paste. After a few seconds add salt, turmeric and red chilli powder. Add the coriander and mint leaves. Sprinkle a little water so that the ingredients can blend better. Add the keema and mix. Stir fry for about 5–6 minutes.

Add the fenugreek leaves and fry for another 5 minutes. Add about ½ glass of water and cook covered on medium-low flame for about 7–8 minutes, till the keema is cooked.

Add the previously boiled lentils and mix gently. Cover and cook for 3–4 minutes. Add the lime juice and turn off the flame.

This is a somewhat-dryish dish.

Serve hot. Goes well with bread, paratha or puri.

THIKRI KI DAL

PREPARATION TIME
10 minutes

COOKING TIME
40 minutes

SERVES
6–8

This is a unique and rather special recipe from Hyderabad. The combination of ghee, red and green chillies and the great herb—fresh green coriander—make it ever so flavourful. But what makes it special is the baghar of 3–4 broken pieces of earthen saucers and heated over charcoal or gas till they burn red, which are then immersed in the lentils. This dish is ideal as a part of a special meal, when you want to impress your guests.

. . . .

- 300 g red gram lentils (masoor dal)
- ⅓rd tsp turmeric powder
- 1 tsp red chilli powder
- 4 tbsp ghee
- 2 onions, finely sliced
- 4 green chillies, hand broken in two
- A few sprigs of fresh green coriander, coarsely chopped
- Juice of 1–2 limes
- Salt

BAGHAR
- 4–5 tbsp ghee
- ½ tsp cumin seeds
- 8–10 cloves of garlic, crushed
- 5 dry red chillies, whole
- ¼th tsp fenugreek seeds
- 25 curry leaves
- 3–4 3-inch pieces broken from fresh earthen saucers (These are generally used to serve an Indian desert called Phirni.)

Boil the lentils in 3½–4 glasses of water, along with salt, turmeric and red chilli powder. When half cooked, add 1 tbsp ghee. Cook till tender.

Separately, heat the remaining ghee. Fry the onions till golden. Add to the lentils. Also add green chillies and coriander. Cook for 5 minutes over medium heat.

For the baghar, heat the ghee. Add cumin seeds. When they get light brown, add garlic and fry till golden. Then add the whole red chillies. When the chillies darken, add the fenugreek seeds, followed by the curry leaves. After about 15 seconds, pour the baghar over the lentils and cover immediately.

Wash the earthen saucer pieces well before heating them over burning charcoal or gas till they are flaming red. Put the pieces into the lentil dish and cover immediately to capture the aroma.

Serve hot with just 2 earthen saucer pieces in the lentils. Remove the extra pieces.

Squeeze the juice of lime before serving.

KHATTI DAL

PREPARATION TIME
10 minutes

COOKING TIME
25 minutes

SERVES
6

- 250 g red gram lentils (arhar dal)
- ⅓rd tsp turmeric powder
- 1 tsp red chilli powder
- 60 g tamarind, washed and soaked in warm water for 10 minutes and strained to get tamarind juice
- Salt

BAGHAR
- 3 tbsp ghee
- 1 heaped tsp cumin seeds
- 10–12 garlic cloves, crushed
- 7–8 dry red chillies
- 15–20 curry leaves

An all-time favourite. A classic dal from Hyderabad. Simple to make and super delicious.

. . . .

Wash and soak the lentils in 4 glasses of water for about 20 minutes. Drain the water.

Place the lentils in a pressure cooker along with salt, turmeric, red chilli powder and 3 glasses of water. Pressure cook till 1–2 whistles. Turn off the heat. Open the lid when the pressure subsides. The lentils at this stage should be tender.

Now add the tamarind juice and cook further for 5 minutes.

For the baghar, heat the ghee. And add cumin seeds. Once they turn rich brown, add crushed garlic. When the garlic turns golden brown add the dry red chillies. As soon as the red chillies turn a rich brown, add the curry leaves. Mix it well. After 10 seconds, pour the baghar over the lentils, mix and immediately cover to capture the aroma.

Serve hot with steaming hot plain rice.

KHAJOOR KA HALWA
WITH CHANE KI DAL

PREPARATION TIME
10 minutes

COOKING TIME
50 minutes

SERVES
10–15

- 250 g Bengal gram lentils, split and skinned (chana dal)
- 1½ kg milk (approx 1500 ml)
- ½ kg fresh dates
- 1½ cup ghee
- 1 tbsp sugar (optional)
- 4 tbsp screwpine flower water (kewda)
- Seeds of 8 green cardamom pods, crushed
- 10–15 almonds, blanched, peeled and slivered
- 10–15 pistachios
- 4–5 silver leaves (chandi ke varq)

An exotic dessert from Hyderabad where chana dal, milk, dates and ghee. The screwpine flower water lends a fragrant touch.

Wash and soak the lentils in 4 glasses of water for 30 minutes. Drain the water.

Boil the lentils along with milk till tender and the liquid dries up. When cool, grind the lentils to a paste.

Wash and deseed the dates. Slice them into slivers. Mash the dates and mix them with the lentils.

Heat the ghee in a heavy-base pan. Add the dates and lentil mixture and fry till well blended. Add sugar, if necessary. Add screwpine water and crushed cardamoms.

Transfer to a nice serving dish and decorate with almonds, pistachio and silver leaves.

KOOTU

PREPARATION TIME
20 minutes

COOKING TIME
30 minutes

SERVES
6–8

- 200 g Bengal gram lentils, split and skinned (chana dal)
- 100 g french beans, cut into small pieces
- 1–2 carrots, cut into small pieces
- 100 g cabbage, sliced thick
- ⅓rd tsp turmeric powder
- ½ tsp red chilli powder
- 2–3 green chillies, slit
- ½ cup fresh finely grated coconut
- 1 tsp cumin powder
- Salt

BAGHAR
- 3 tbsp oil
- 1 tsp black gram lentils, split and skinned (urad dal, dhuli)
- ½ tsp mustard seed
- 2–3 dry red chillies, broken
- 15–20 curry leaves

Kootu is any one vegetable or a medley of fresh vegetables cooked with lentils and tempered. This one uses French beans, carrots, and cabbage, and is cooked with split gram lentils. Fresh grated coconut lends both richness and ever-so-gentle creaminess. A staple food, found in most Tamil homes.

Wash and soak the lentils in about 2 glasses of water for 30 minutes. Drain the water.

Place the lentils in a pressure cooker. Add 2 glasses of water and cook till 2 whistles. Lower the heat and cook further for 3–4 minutes. Open the lid when the pressure subsides. The lentils should be tender. When done, there should be 2–3 tbsp water left in the lentils. Otherwise add 2–3 tbsp hot water. Set aside.

Put all the vegetables into another heavy-base, wide pan. Add the salt, turmeric, red chilli powder and green chillies. Add 1 cup water and bring the dish to a steaming point. Then lower the heat and cook for about 7–8 minutes till the vegetables are tender. Add the previously boiled lentils to the vegetables. Cook first on a high flame till the dish is steaming again. Add the grated coconut, keeping 1 tbsp aside for garnishing later, and cumin powder. Mix gently and simmer for 5 minutes.

Heat the oil for the baghar. Add urad dal, followed after a few seconds by mustard seeds. When mustard starts to splutter and the urad dal turns red brown, add dry red chillies followed in a few seconds by the curry leaves. When the chillies darken, pour the baghar over the lentil dish. Mix gently.

Serve hot, garnished with the grated coconut.

MIXED DAL RASAM

PREPARATION TIME
5 minutes

COOKING TIME
25–30 minutes

SERVES
6–8

An invigorating mixed dal Rasam from Tamil Nadu. Deliciously flavoured with aromatic spices. The seasoning with ghee, red chillies and curry leaves enhances the flavours dramatically.

. . . .

- 150 g red gram lentils, red lentils, split gram lentils and yellow lentils in equal proportion (arhar, masoor, chana and moong dal, dhuli)
- ⅓rd tsp turmeric powder
- 50 g tamarind
- 1 tbsp oil
- 2 tbsp coriander seeds
- 5–6 dry whole red chillies
- 10 peppercorns
- A pinch of asafoetida
- 3–4 tomatoes, skinned and chopped into medium-sized pieces and lightly mashed
- Salt

BAGHAR
- 2 tbsp ghee
- 5–6 cashew nuts, broken
- 1 tbsp peanuts
- 2–3 dry whole red chillies
- A few curry leaves

Wash and soak all the lentils together in 3–4 glasses of water for 30 minutes. Drain. Cook the lentils in about 3 glasses of water together with turmeric, till each grain is tender. Mash, sieve, and set aside.

Wash and soak the tamarind in one cup of warm water for 15 minutes. Mash and sieve to get tamarind juice. Set aside.

Heat the oil in a pan. Add coriander seeds and fry till golden. Add red chillies, peppercorns and then asafoetida. Immediately remove the pan from the heat, and allow it to cool. Grind this mixture into a powder.

In a separate vessel, add one glass of water to the tamarind juice, and bring it to a boil. Add salt, ground spices and tomatoes to the tamarind water and cook on a medium flame for about 5 minutes. Add the previously boiled lentils, mix and cook further for 6–7 minutes.

Heat the ghee. Fry the cashew nuts and peanuts till they are golden. Remove. Add red chillies to the ghee. When the chillies darken, add curry leaves. In a few seconds, pour the baghar, along with the cashew nuts and peanuts (after removing skin) over the rasam.

Serve hot.

ARHAR DAL WITH VEGETABLES

PREPARATION TIME
20 minutes

COOKING TIME
30 minutes

SERVES
6

- 200 g red gram lentils (arhar dal)
- ¼th tsp turmeric powder
- 50 g tamarind
- 55 ml oil
- ½ tsp mustard seeds
- 1 tsp cumin seeds
- 2 bay leaves
- 3–4 dry red whole chillies
- A pinch of asafoetida
- A few curry leaves
- 2 small onions, sliced
- 2 carrots
- 100 g French beans } cut into 1½-inch sized pieces
- 1 radish
- 2 drumsticks, cut into 2-inch sized pieces
- 100 g okra, whole and stem cut
- 1 tsp red chilli powder
- 1 tsp coriander powder
- ½ tsp cumin powder
- 20 g jaggery
- A few sprigs of fresh green coriander, chopped
- Salt

A medley of vegetables, cooked with arhar dal, this dish from Tamil Nadu is somewhat in the nature of sambhar. And almost any seasonal vegetables can be used. Gently sweet and sour, this is delicious and flavoursome.

. . . .

Wash and soak the lentils for about 20 minutes. Drain and wash afresh. In a heavy-base pan, place the lentils, add 3½ glasses of water and turmeric powder. Cook the lentils first on a high flame and then on medium-low flame, partially covered. Cook till tender.

Wash and soak tamarind in one cup of warm water. Mash and sieve to extract tamarind juice. Set aside.

Heat the oil in a heavy-base pan. Add mustard seeds, followed by cumin seeds, bay leaves and red chillies. In just 5 seconds, add the asafoetida and curry leaves, immediately followed by the onions. When the onions turn translucent, add the carrot, radish, okra, French beans and drumsticks. Fry for 5–7 minutes.

Add the already cooked lentils to the vegetables. Also add chilli, coriander powder, cumin powder, salt and the tamarind juice. Add jaggery and cook covered on a medium flame for about 5–6 minutes. Lastly add the fresh green coriander.

Serve hot.

TORI AUR MOONG DHULI DAL

PREPARATION TIME
10 minutes

COOKING TIME
25 minutes

SERVES
6-8

- 200 g green gram lentils, split and skinned (moong dal, dhuli)
- ⅓rd tsp turmeric powder
- 6–8 ridge gourds
- 2 tbsp oil
- 1 tsp mustard seeds
- 1 tsp cumin seeds
- 3–4 dry whole red chillies, broken
- 15–20 curry leaves
- 2–3 green chillies, hand broken into 2 each
- ½ tsp freshly crushed pepper
- 1 tbsp ghee
- Salt

The ever-so-gentle flavour of the moong dhuli dal, together with the mild sweetness of the ridge gourd makes this a light and refreshing dish, which is also easily digested.

. . . .

Wash and soak the lentils in water for 20 minutes. Drain the water. Boil the lentils in 2½ glasses of water along with the turmeric powder till tender. Lightly mash and set aside.

Scrape and chop the gourds into medium-sized pieces. Dip in water and set aside.

Heat the oil in a separate heavy-base pan. Add mustard seeds. When the seeds start to splutter, add cumin seeds, followed by dry whole red chillies a few seconds later. When the chillies are reddish brown, add the curry leaves. Next add the chopped gourd and mix. Reduce the flame to medium and stir fry for 5 minutes.

Add the previously boiled lentils and salt, and cook covered on a medium flame. Cook till the gourds are tender. Add green chillies, pepper and ghee, and turn off the flame.

This dal has medium-thick consistency.

Serve hot.

TOMATO RASAM

PREPARATION TIME
10–15 minutes

COOKING TIME
30 minutes

SERVES
6–8

- 200 g red lentils (masoor dal)
- ⅓rd tsp turmeric
- 55 ml oil
- ½ tsp mustard oil
- 1 tsp cumin seeds
- 15–20 curry leaves
- A pinch of asafoetida (optional)
- 4 tomatoes, pureed
- 4 tomatoes chopped into medium pieces
- 3 green chillies, slit down the middle
- 1 tbsp ginger, sliced.
- 1 onion cut into medium-sized pieces
- ⅓rd cup, fresh green coriander, chopped
- 60 g jaggery
- Juice of 1½–2 limes
- Salt

This dish gives instant joy. The fragrant blend of ginger, green chillies, and curry leaves together with tomatoes makes this dish ever so enticing. Jaggery and lime together take the flavours to another level.

It is soupy in texture and has a sweet and sour flavour.

. . . .

Wash and soak the lentils in 4 glasses of water for 20 minutes. Drain the water.

Place the lentils in a pressure cooker with 4 glasses of water, salt and turmeric. Pressure cook till 2 whistles and turn off the flame. Open the pressure cooker when the pressure subsides. The lentils at this stage should be tender.

Heat the oil in a heavy-base pan. Add mustard seeds, followed in a few seconds by cumin seeds. When mustard starts to pop add the curry leaves and asafoetida. Then add the tomato puree and cook for about 4–5 minutes. Next add the chopped tomatoes and cook for another 4–5 minutes. Now add 2 green chillies, half of the ginger, onion, and fresh coriander. Stir fry for 1–2 minutes and add the previously boiled lentils. Bring the lentils to a boil. Add the jaggery and the balance onion and cook further for 2–3 minutes. As the dish is medium-thin in consistency, add a little water if necessary.

Now add the balance of green chillies, ginger and fresh green coriander. Turn off the flame. Squeeze the juice of lime and mix.

Serve hot with steaming hot rice.

SPICY MOONG DAL WITH VEGETABLES

PREPARATION TIME
15 minutes

COOKING TIME
25-30 minutes

SERVES
6

- 200 g green gram lentils, split and skinned (moong dal, dhuli)
- ⅓rd tsp turmeric powder
- 1 potato, diced into small pieces
- 100 g French beans, cut into small pieces
- 100 g cauliflower, cut into small florets
- 65 ml oil
- ¼th tsp nigella seeds (kalonji)
- ¼th tsp caraway seeds (shah jeera)
- 1 onion, sliced
- 1½ inch piece of ginger, chopped
- 5–6 cloves of garlic, chopped
- 4–5 dry red chillies
- 1 tsp chilli powder
- Salt

GARNISH
- A few sprigs of fresh coriander
- 2–3 green chillies, chopped

This spicy moong dal, full of flavour, can be served as a part of any meal, daily or special and will also make a nice breakfast item with toast. Seasonal vegetables such as carrots and peas can also be used, substituting one or two others. You have to try it to know how good it is.

Wash and soak the lentils in 3 glasses of water for 20 minutes. Drain the water.

Boil the lentils in 2 glasses of water with salt and turmeric, first on a high flame, and then partially covered on a medium-low flame till tender but not mushy. There should be sufficient moisture left when done.

Blanch the vegetables i.e., plunge them in boiling water for just 30 seconds. Strain the water and set aside.

Heat the oil. Add the nigella and caraway seeds immediately followed by the onion. As the onion turns pink, add ginger and garlic, and fry till the onion becomes golden brown. Add the dry red chillies. When the chillies turn dark red, add the chilli powder, followed immediately by the blanched vegetables. Cook for about 6–7 minutes, sprinkling a little water if needed.

When the vegetables turn soft, add the previously cooked lentils. Sprinkle a little water, if necessary, as the dish should not be too dry and must retain a hint of moisture. Cook for just about 2 minutes.

Serve hot, garnished with fresh coriander and green chillies

CHANA DAL

PREPARATION TIME
5 minutes

COOKING TIME
15–20 minutes

SERVES
6–8

- 150 g Bengal gram lentils, split and skinned (chana dal)
- 1 tsp crushed pepper
- A few sprigs of fresh green coriander
- Juice of 1 lime
- Salt

How simple can simple get. Yet, the crushed pepper, fresh green coriander and the refreshing citrus flavour of fresh lime make this dish ever so delicious.

Wash and soak the lentils in water for 1 hour. Drain the water.

Boil the lentils with salt and 1 glass of water till tender. When done, each grain should be tender and separate, and no water left in the pan.

Add crushed pepper, fresh coriander and lime juice. Mix and serve.

Can serve both as a snack or a side dish with the main course.

PAYASAM

PREPARATION TIME
10 minutes

COOKING TIME
25 minutes

SERVES
6–8

- 100 g green gram lentils, split and skinned (moong dal, dhuli)
- 75 g jaggery
- Seeds of 6 green cardamom pods, powdered
- A pinch of saffron
- 1 cup milk

Moong dal with jaggery, flavoured with cardamom and saffron. Usually, it is offered in most south Indian temples as prasad.

. . . .

Wash and soak the lentils for 30 minutes. Drain the water.

Add 1½ glasses of water to the lentils and boil till tender. Mash.

Separately boil the jaggery in ½ glass of water till it melts. Sieve through a fine strainer to remove any sediments and impurities and add to the cooked lentils. Heat the lentils till just one boil. Also add the powdered cardamoms. Add saffron to a cup of warm milk and add to the lentils. Cook for another 30 seconds.

This is a somewhat soupy dish. Serve hot. Can be used as a dessert and served in small bowls.

A SPICE-FLAVOURED KERALA DAL

PREPARATION TIME
15 minutes

COOKING TIME
30 minutes

SERVES
6–8

- 200 g ochre lentils (masoor dal, sabut)
- ⅓rd tsp turmeric powder
- 3–4 cloves
- 2–3 green cardamom pods
- 1 inch cinnamon stick
- 1 tsp fennel seeds

A

- 55 ml oil
- 1 tsp mustard seeds
- A few curry leaves
- 1 tsp ginger crushed
- 3–4 cloves of garlic, crushed
- 6 green chillies, slit down the middle
- 3 tbsp shallots, cut into fine rings
- 1 large tomato, chopped
- Salt

Kerala is the spice garden of India. This dal brings out the full flavours of spices grown in the state. Green chillies and shallots further enhance its flavour.

Wash and soak the lentils in 3 glasses of water for 30 minutes. Drain the water just before cooking.

Place the lentils in a pressure cooker. Add 2½ glasses of water and a little salt. Pressure cook till 1–2 whistles. When the steam subsides, uncover and check that the lentils are tender.

Grind together all the spices at 'A' with a little water to a fine paste. Set aside.

Heat the oil. Add mustard seeds. When they start to splutter, add curry leaves, followed by ginger and garlic. Add the ground masala and salt, and sauté for one minute. Add green chillies and shallots and fry for another 1–2 minutes. Then add the tomato. Fry till the tomato turns soft and oil starts to surface. Pour the contents into the boiled lentils. Mix and cook for 4–5 minutes for the contents to blend.

This dish has medium-thick consistency.

Serve hot. Goes well with steaming hot rice, puri or roti.

MASOOR DAL AND BITTER GOURD THEEYAL

PREPARATION TIME
20 minutes

COOKING TIME
40 minutes

SERVES
6

- 150 g red lentils (masoor dal)
- ⅔rd tsp turmeric powder
- 200 g bitter gourd
- 2 tbsp tamarind pulp
- 2 tbsp oil
- 2 tbsp Bengal gram lentils, split and skinned (chana dal)
- 30 g desiccated coconut, grated
- 1 tbsp coriander seeds
- ¼th tsp fenugreek seeds
- 10 dry red chillies
- A pinch of asafoetida
- Salt

} A

BAGHAR
- 2 tbsp oil
- 1 tsp mustard seeds
- 1 tsp sesame seeds
- 1 tbsp shallots, sliced fine
- A few curry leaves

Hot, aromatic and flavourful, this dish from Kerala is a real treat. Theeyal can also be made using a variety of other vegetables, such as button onions, eggplant, okra, zucchini and raw mango, individually or in combination.

Wash and soak the lentils in 3 glasses of water for 30 minutes. Drain the water.

Take a heavy-base pan. Place the lentils in the pan. Add 2½ glasses of water, half of the turmeric and cook covered, first on a high flame and then medium-low till tender. Set aside.

Meanwhile, lightly scrape the bitter gourd and cut into 1½-inch-long pieces. Remove any large seeds. Add a little salt, rub with your hands and set aside for about 10 minutes. After 10 minutes, squeeze out the water from the bitter gourd and wash them.

Add 1½ glasses of water to the bitter gourd. Also add tamarind pulp and the balance turmeric powder and cook till the bitter gourd is almost tender. Simultaneously heat oil in a separate pan. Add all the ingredients at 'A' and lightly fry them till they start to give a fragrant aroma. Using a little water, grind the mixture into a fine paste.

Now add salt, bitter gourd and the ground masala into the dal. Mix and simmer for about 5 minutes.

For the baghar, heat oil. Add mustard seeds, followed by sesame seeds after a few seconds. When the mustard seeds start to splutter, add the shallot and curry leaves. After about 1 minute, add the baghar to the lentils.

This dish has medium-thick consistency. Serve hot.

PAYAR THENGA

PREPARATION TIME
20 minutes

COOKING TIME
30 minutes

SERVES
6–8

Coconut and baby onions, cooked together with the lentils, impart a soothing mild sweetness to this dish. The flavour is considerably enhanced by the tempering, using coconut oil, red chillies and curry leaves.

- 100 g red gram lentils (arhar dal)
- 100 g green gram lentils, split and skinned (moong dal, dhuli)
- ⅓rd tsp turmeric powder
- 1 tsp red chilli powder
- ¼th tsp asafoetida
- 1½ inch piece ginger ⎫ ground to
- 5–6 cloves of garlic ⎭ a paste
- 100 g fresh coconut, sliced
- 100 g baby onions, peeled
- Salt

BAGHAR
- 2 tbsp coconut oil
- 1 tsp mustard seeds
- 3–4 dry red chillies, broken
- 15–20 curry leaves

Wash and soak the lentils together in 3½ glasses of water for 30 minutes.

Drain, wash and place the lentils in a heavy-bottom pan. Add 3 glasses of water and the listed ingredients till the baby onions and salt. Bring the lentils to a boil on high flame and then lower the flame and cook covered till tender.

Heat the coconut oil. Add the mustard seeds. When they start to splutter, add red chillies, followed in about 5 seconds by curry leaves. When the chillies darken, pour the baghar over the cooked lentils. Mix and cook on medium-low flame for 3–4 minutes.

This dish has medium consistency.

Serve hot.

RASAM, KERALA-STYLE

PREPARATION TIME
10–15 minutes

COOKING TIME
30 minutes

SERVES
8

Much of Kerala is coastal and abounds in spices, coconut, fish and prawns. It is but natural that these ingredients form an integral part of Kerala cuisine.

Rasam is common to most South Indian states. More soupy in nature, Rasam is usually had with boiled rice. This Rasam from Kerala uses many aromatic spices, and combined with fresh herbs, shallots, and the juice of fresh lime, the result is fantastic.

. . . .

- 150 g red lentils (masoor dal, dhuli)
- ½ tsp turmeric powder
- ½ tsp peppercorns, crushed
- 1 inch cinnamon stick
- 6 cloves
- 1 tsp ghee

} A

- 1 medium onion, cut into 4–6 pieces each
- 3 large tomatoes (250 g) each cut into 4–5 pieces
- 1 tbsp coriander seeds
- 6 cloves of garlic
- ½ tsp sugar
- Juice of 2 limes
- A few sprigs of fresh green coriander

BAGHAR
- 2 tbsp oil
- 1 tsp mustard seeds
- ½ tsp cumin seeds
- 4 dry red chillies
- 1 tbsp shallots, sliced into fine rings

Wash and soak the lentils in 3 glasses of water for 30 minutes. Drain the water.

Place the lentils in a heavy pan. Add 2½–3 glasses of water. Also add all the ingredients at 'A'. Cook first on a high flame, covered till the lentils come to a boil. Then reduce the flame to medium-low and cook the lentils till half done. Add salt, onion and tomato, and cook till the lentils are tender. Mash with a wooden spoon.

Coarsely crush the coriander seeds and garlic. Boil in one glass of water for 3 minutes. Strain and add the water to the rasam. Add a little more water if necessary as rasam has somewhat thin consistency. Boil for another 2–3 minutes. Add sugar, lime juice and fresh coriander.

Heat the oil for the baghar. Add mustard seeds, followed in a few seconds by cumin seeds. When the mustard starts to splutter and cumin seeds turn light brown, add red chillies. When the chillies darken, add shallots. Sauté for about a minute or so. Add the baghar to the rasam.

Serve hot with a meal in small glass bowls. Goes well with rice and papad.

RASAM KERALA-STYLE

MURINGAKAI THEEYAL

PREPARATION TIME
20 minutes

COOKING TIME
30 minutes

SERVES
6–8

* 100 g red lentils
  (masoor dal, dhuli)
* 100 g red gram lentils
  (arhar dal)
* 2 tbsp Bengal gram
  lentils, split and
  skinned (chana dal)
* 4–5 drumsticks cut
  into 3-inch pieces
* ½ cup fresh coconut,
  grated
* 4–5 dry red chillies ⎫
* 1½ tbsp coriander │
  seeds │
* 15–20 curry leaves ⎬ A
* ½ tsp peppercorns │
* ½ tsp cumin seeds │
* ¼th tsp asafoetida ⎭
* 2 tbsp coconut oil
* 100 g baby onions,
  peeled
* 2 tbsp tamarind pulp
* 1 tbsp jaggery,
  crushed
* Salt

BAGHAR

* 2 tbsp coconut oil
* 1 tsp mustard seeds
* 2–3 red chillies,
  broken

Another traditional treat from Kerala. Roasted spices together with the signature sweetness of coconut lend this dish an amazing flavour.

Wash and soak all the three lentils together in 3 glasses of water for 30 minutes.

Drain the water. Place the lentils in a heavy-base pan. Add 3 glasses of hot water. Bring the lentils to a boil on high flame. Reduce the heat and cook the lentils covered till tender. Set aside.

Boil the drumsticks in one glass of water till almost tender. Set aside.

Dry roast the coconut in a pan till pale gold. Remove and set aside. Now dry roast all the ingredients at 'A' till a fine aroma starts to emanate. Do not brown the ingredients. Now add a little water and grind all the ingredients together with the coconut to a fine paste.

Now start heating the previously boiled lentils. Separately heat the coconut oil in a pan. Add onions and sauté for 2 minutes. Add the onions to the lentils. Also add the drumsticks with the water in which they were boiled. Add and mix the ground paste. Also add salt, tamarind and jaggery.

Mix and cook covered on a medium flame for 5 minutes.

Heat the oil for the baghar. Add mustard seeds. When they start to sizzle, add the red chillies. When mustard seeds start to splutter, add the shallot and curry leaves. After about 1 minute, add the baghar to the lentils.

This dish has medium-thick consistency. Serve hot.

KERALA PARIPPU CURRY

PREPARATION TIME
10–15 minutes

COOKING TIME
25 minutes

SERVES
6

Served during the festive occasion of Onam to celebrate the harvest season, it is a favourite that is also made regularly in Kerala homes. Coconut and spices, together with ghee, make this a truly delicious treat.

* 150 g green gram lentils, split and skinned (moong dal, dhuli)
* ⅓rd tsp turmeric powder
* ½ cup fresh coconut, grated
* 3 green chillies, chopped
* 1 shallot, sliced
* Salt

ground to a paste

BAGHAR
* 3 tbsp ghee
* ½ tsp mustard seeds
* 3–4 dry whole red chillies, each broken into 2–3 pieces
* 15–20 curry leaves
* 1 shallot, sliced

Roast the lentils in a heavy-base pan till they turn a rich golden colour. Wash and pressure cook the lentils with turmeric in 2½–3 glasses of water. Pressure took till 2 whistles.

Open when the pressure subsides. The lentils should be tender at this stage. If not, cook a little more without pressure till tender. Mash the lentils with a masher or a wooden churner (madhani). Add salt and the ground paste to the lentils. Cook for 6–7 minutes till well blended.

For the baghar, heat 2 tbsp ghee. Add mustard seeds. When the seeds start to splutter, add red chillies. When the chillies darken, add the curry leaves and the shallot. Once the shallot turns golden, pour the baghar over the lentils and mix. Drizzle 1 tbsp ghee over the lentils before serving.

Serve hot. Goes well with hot steamed rice, papad and pickle of your choice.

BISI BELE HULIYANA

PREPARATION TIME
10–15 minutes

COOKING TIME
30 minutes

SERVES
6–8

A famous and traditional recipe from Karnataka, it is cooked in most Kannada homes.

Utterly delectable, this dish is an unbelievable medley of lentils, rice and a host of vegetables. The flavour is perked up with the use of tamarind, coconut, a variety of spices and ghee.

. . . .

- 150 g red lentils or red gram lentils (masoor dal or arhar dal)
- 100 g rice
- 50 g tamarind
- 6–8 dry red chillies ⎫
- 25 g desiccated coconut ⎪
- 1 tsp red gram lentils (arhar dal) ⎪
- 1 tsp black gram lentils (urad dal, dhuli) ⎬ A
- ½ tsp fenugreek seeds ⎪
- 1 tbsp coriander seeds ⎪
- 1 tsp aniseeds ⎭
- 2 brinjals
- 1 carrot
- 50 g peeled peas
- 1 potato
- 100 g button onions, peeled
- 2–3 tbsp oil
- ¼th tsp turmeric powder
- Salt

BAGHAR
- 1 tbsp ghee
- 2 tbsp oil
- 1 tsp mustard seeds
- 4–5 dry red chillies
- 15–20 curry leaves
- A pinch of asafoetida
- Salt

Soak the lentils and rice together for 20 minutes.

Soak tamarind in 1 cup warm water, mash and strain to get tamarind juice. Keep aside.

Lightly dry roast all the spices at 'A'. Grind them in a mixie to a powder-like consistency.

Chop all the vegetables into small pieces. Let the baby onions remain whole. Heat the oil. Fry all the vegetables lightly. Set aside.

Drain the soaked rice and the lentils. Place them in a pressure cooker with 2½–3 glasses of water, salt and turmeric powder. Pressure cook till 1–2 whistles. Reduce the flame and cook for another 2 minutes before taking it off the heat. Turn off the flame. Allow the steam to subside. Uncover Add tamarind juice, the ground spices and the vegetables. Cook till the rice and lentils are tender and the contents well blended.

For the baghar, heat the ghee and the oil. Add mustard seeds followed by red chillies. When the mustard seeds splutter and the chillies darken, add the curry leaves and asafoetida. In a few seconds, pour the baghar over Bisi Bele Huliyana, mix and cover.

Serve hot.

BISI BELE HULIYANA

East

EAST

East India comprises the states of West Bengal, Assam, Odisha, Bihar and Jharkhand, among others.

WEST BENGAL, ASSAM, BIHAR AND JHARKHAND

Surrounded by rivers and the ocean, east India focuses on fresh fish. Hilsa, promfret, bhetki, shrimp, prawn and crabs are all used with abandon. Vegetables and fruits are grown in abundance. Lentil dishes are made along with fish and vegetables, and served with rice. Simplicity and moderate use of spices characterize the cuisine of the east.

When it comes to greens, Bengalis are known for using every part of the vegetables and turning them into most sumptuous dishes.

The cooking medium of West Bengal is mustard oil, adding a pungent and slightly sweet flavour. Punchpuran, a combination of five spices i.e., nigella, fennel, cumin, mustard and fenugreek, is used liberally for tempering.

West Bengal is renowned for its sweets—Rasgullas, Sandesh, Rasmalai and Payesh (a rice pudding sweetened with jaggery).

Kolkata is also famous for its street food. Phuchka (popularly known as Golgappa in north India) is hugely popular. Jhal-Muri (spicy puffed rice) just tossed with green chillies, chopped onions, peanuts, lime juice and mustard oil is another favourite food. When my father was posted in Kolkata, and I was a young child, I remember walking with my mother and younger sister from Hindustan Park, where we were staying, to the nearby lake and along the way eating Jhal-Muri sold in newspaper cones.
I still remember the flavour with nostalgia.

Now one finds momos and biryanis being sold as street food along with Jhal-Muri and Phuchkas.

West Bengal has been exposed to different culinary influences—Mughal, Chinese and British. The Bengali cuisine has, thus, emerged embracing these influences, yet retaining its own identity.

Since Jharkhand was earlier a part of the state of Bihar, it shares many similarities with Bihari cuisine. It's also famous for its tribal food. Included in this section are some flavoursome dals such as Khatti Meethi Chane ki Dal, Chana Dal, Bengali-style, a simple but nutritious Mati Maa Dal from Assam, Jharkhand Chane ki Dal and Moong Dal Halwa from Bihar.

JHARKHAND KI CHANE KI DAL

PREPARATION TIME
20 minutes

COOKING TIME
30 minutes

SERVES
6–8

Jharkhand, earlier a part of Bihar, shares some similarities with Bihari cuisine. However, it is famous for its tribal food, often found in tribal villages or at weddings.

Here is a traditional chana dal from Jharkhand. The blend of spices, together with fresh coconut, ghee and unsalted butter add richness to the dish.

- 200 g Bengal gram lentils, split and skinned (chana dal)
- 2 tbsp green gram lentils, split and skinned (moong dal, dhuli)
- ⅓rd tsp turmeric powder ⎫
- 1 tbsp ginger paste
- 1 onion, chopped
- 1 tomato, chopped
- 2 tbsp fresh coconut, chopped ⎬ A
- 1 bay leaf
- ½ tsp peppercorns
- 2 black cardamoms
- 2–3 green cardamoms ⎭
- Oil to fry
- 2 onions, sliced
- Salt

BAGHAR
- 1 tbsp ghee
- 1 tsp cumin seeds
- A pinch of asafoetida
- 1 tbsp unsalted butter

Wash and soak chana and moong dal in 3 glasses of water for 1 hour. Drain the water and wash again.

Place the lentils in a heavy-base pan. Add all the ingredients at 'A' along with salt. Add 3½ glasses of water and cook covered, first on high flame till the lentils come to a boil and then on medium-low flame till the lentils are tender.

Meanwhile, heat the oil. Fry the onions till they are golden brown. Set aside.

For baghar, heat the ghee. Add cumin seeds to it. When the cumin seeds turn golden brown, add asafoetida. Immediately pour this baghar over the lentils, together with the fried onions, and mix.

Garnish with unsalted butter and serve hot.

CHANA DAL, BENGALI-STYLE

PREPARATION TIME
10 minutes

COOKING TIME
35–40 minutes

SERVES
6–8

- 250 g Bengal gram lentils, split and skinned (chana dal)
- ⅓rd tsp turmeric
- 2½ tbsp ghee
- 2 tbsp desiccated coconut, chopped into thin, small pieces
- 1 tbsp cashew nuts
- 1 tbsp rasins
- 2 bay leaves
- ½ tsp cumin seeds
- 3–4 cloves
- 1½ inch cinnamon stick
- 3–4 green cardamom pods
- 1 tbsp ginger paste
- 2–3 green chillies, chopped
- 2 tsp sugar
- ½ tsp garam masala
- Salt

X

Sweet and rich, this is an incredibly simple and tasty dal from West Bengal. Split gram lentils give this dish a naturally earthy flavour. And a host of aromatic spices, including garam masala, together with coconut, raisins and ghee make it sublime.

Wash and soak the lentils for 30 minutes in water 3–4 inches above the surface of the lentils. Drain the water after 30 minutes.

Place the lentils in a pressure cooker along with salt, turmeric, 3 glasses of water and pressure cook on high flame till 2 whistles. Reduce the heat to low and cook for another 2–3 minutes. When the pressure subsides, uncover. When done, the lentils should be tender and should not get mushy.

Now heat the ghee in a pan. Fry the coconut pieces and cashew nuts till they turn pink. Remove and set aside. Next fry the raisins. When they swell, remove and place them along with the coconut and cashew nuts. In the same ghee, add all the ingredients at 'X'. After 5 seconds, add the ginger paste and green chillies. Fry for about 10 seconds. Then add this baghar to the previously boiled lentils along with coconut, cashew and raisins. Also add the sugar and garam masala. Mix and cook covered for 10 minutes.

The dish has medium-thick consistency. Goes well with poori, parantha and rice.

KHATTI MEETHI CHANE KI DAL

PREPARATION TIME
10 minutes

COOKING TIME
30 minutes

SERVES
6

Chana dal is one of the most popular dals in Indian cuisine and lends itself to use in myriad ways—soups, salads, dal preparation savouries, sweets and rice dishes.

This Khatti Meethi Chane ki Dal from West Bengal is immensely flavourful with a sweet, spicy and tangy flavour. The name is so derived from the combined use of tamarind, dates and jaggery that peps you up and leaves you wanting more.

· ·

- 200 g Bengal gram lentils, split and skinned (chana dal)
- 2 tbsp green gram lentils, split and skinned (moong dal, dhuli)
- 2 tbsp green gram lentils, whole (moong dal, sabut)
- ⅓rd tsp turmeric powder
- 2 tbsp tamarind pulp
- 3–4 dry red chillies, coarsely ground to a paste
- 1 tsp coriander powder
- 2 dry dates, chopped
- 1–1½ tbsp jaggery
- A few curry leaves
- A few sprigs of fresh green coriander, chopped
- Salt

BAGHAR
- 3 tbsp oil
- ½ tsp mustard seeds
- 1 tsp cumin seeds
- 1 inch cinnamon stick
- 3–4 cloves

Wash and soak the lentils in 4 glasses of water for 1 hour. Drain the water. Wash again.

Add 3½ glasses of water and turmeric, and pressure cook the lentils till 2–3 whistles. Open when the pressure subsides. The lentils should be tender. If not, cook further without pressure till the lentils soften.

Add salt, tamarind pulp, red chilli paste, coriander powder, dry dates, jaggery and curry leaves to the lentils. Cook on medium-low flame for about 10 minutes.

For the baghar, heat the oil. Add mustard seeds, followed by cumin seeds. When the mustard seeds pop and cumin seeds turn golden brown, add cinnamon and cloves. In just 30 seconds, pour the baghar over the lentils. Mix and cover.

Garnish with fresh coriander leaves and serve hot.

ASSAMESE MATI MAA

PREPARATION TIME
15 minutes

COOKING TIME
40 minutes

SERVES
6–8

Black lentils or urad dal has been cultivated in India since ancient times and is widely used in various cuisines in the country.

Made with whole black lentils, Assamese Mati Maa is an earthy, nutritious and a no-fuss dish. The combined use of herbs, chillies and other spices make the flavour of this dish divine. It is an immensely popular dal in Assam.

- 200 g black lentils, whole (urad dal, sabut)
- 2 tomatoes, chopped
- 1 onion, chopped
- ⅓rd tsp turmeric powder
- ½ tsp red chilli powder
- Salt

BAGHAR
- 3 tbsp oil
- 1 bay leaf
- 1 tsp cumin seeds
- 2 dry red chillies
- 1 tbsp chopped ginger
- 1 tbsp chopped garlic
- 2–3 green chillies, chopped

Wash and soak the lentils in 4 glasses of water overnight. Next morning drain the lentils and wash in fresh water.

Place the lentils in a pressure cooker. Add 4 glasses of water, tomatoes, onion, turmeric, red chilli powder and salt. Pressure cook till 1–2 whistles and then simmer on a low flame for about 10 minutes till tender. Uncover when the pressure subsides. The lentils at this stage should be tender. If not, cook a little more without pressure.

In a pan, heat the oil. Add the bay leaf, cumin seeds and red chillies. When the cumin seeds turn golden brown and red chillies red brown add ginger, garlic and green chillies. In about half a minute, pour the baghar over the lentils and mix. Cook for 2–3 minutes.

Serve hot.

MOONG DAL HALWA

PREPARATION TIME
10 minutes

COOKING TIME
35–40 minutes

SERVES
8

- 200 g green gram lentils, split and skinned (moong dal, dhuli)
- 1 cup sugar
- 1 cup milk
- A generous pinch of saffron
- ½ cup dried whole milk (khoya)
- 1 cup ghee
- 1 tbsp gram flour (besan)
- Seeds of 10–12 green cardamom pods, powdered
- 15–20 almonds, sliced
- 3–4 silver leaves (chandi ke varq)

Moong Dal Halwa is perfect for any festival, be it Holi, Diwali or Ganesh Chaturthi. Even though it is a festive indulgence in Bihar, it is cooked and relished in other parts of the country too. It is also often served at weddings and parties.

This halwa is rich and delicious. Winter is a great time to enjoy it.

. . . .

Wash and soak the lentils in 3 glasses of water for at least 6–8 hours. Drain the water and grind the lentils to a coarse paste.

Add 1 cup water to the sugar and heat the mixture till the sugar dissolves. Cook for 2 more minutes and set aside.

Heat the milk and add saffron. Crush the khoya and add to the milk. Cook for 2 minutes. Set aside.

Heat the ghee in a heavy-bottom pan. Add the gram flour and stir for a minute. Then, add the ground lentils and keep stirring to prevent the lentils from sticking to the pan. Sauté on medium-low heat for about 20 minutes till it turns fragrant and golden brown.

Now add the sugar syrup to the lentils and mix well. Next add the saffron milk with khoya and mix well. Cook on a low flame for about 5–10 minutes, stirring occasionally. Sprinkle the cardamom powder on top and mix.

Transfer to a serving dish hot and decorate with almond slivers and chandi ke varq.

West

WEST

Western Indian states, inter-alia, include Maharashtra, Gujarat, Goa and Rajasthan.

MAHARASHTRA

Maharashtrian cuisine includes an enormous variety of vegetables, fish and coconut. Peanuts, cashew nuts, kokum (a deep purple berry with a pleasing sweet and sour taste) and jaggery and tamarind are all commonly used. Rice is the staple food grain in Maharashtra. Jawar and Bajra are also used.

When it comes to food, the land of Maharashtra can never disappoint you. From the spicy Kolhapuri Mutton and world-famous Pao Bhaji to delicious Poha (a snack made of flattened rice and Bhelpuri) which is a savoury snack—you have it all! Puranpoli is a sweet version of the parantha made with chana dal and jaggery. Bombay Duck is a delight for the non-vegetarians.

Some of the famous dals included in this section are Lentils in Coconut Milk, Katachi Amti, Moong Usal, Puranpoli and more.

GOA

Located on the shore of the Arabian sea, Goa has an irresistible charm, what with its lovely beaches and coconut palms. Goan food is considered incomplete without fish and prawns. Ingredients such as coconut, chillies, toddy vinegar, kokum and tamarind dominate the Goan cuisine. On account of 450 years of Portuguese civilization, Goan cuisine is quite influenced by the Portuguese cuisine. Local dishes like Vindaloo and Xacuti testify to the fact.

Included in the following section are two lovely dals from Goa—Goan Dal Masala and Coconut and Chilli Lentils.

GUJARAT

Gujarat is essentially a vegetarian state due to the influence of Hindu and Jain religions.

Many communities, however, do include seafood, mutton and chicken in their food.

The Gujarati Thali is an experience to try. It consists of various dals, Karhi (a yoghurt-based dish with vegetable fritters) and a variety of vegetables. Flavours can be sweet, spicy and sour. Khandvi, Dhokla, Thepla and Dhebra are some amazing dishes that the state offers and are highly popular.

This section includes Khichra, an amazing mix of lentils, meat and spices and favoured by the Muslims and Parsis. It also includes a Parsi dish called Dhansak, a great dal and meat dish. Angoor ki Dal is yet another flavourful dish.

RAJASTHAN

Rajasthan lies largely in the dry stretches of Thar Desert where fresh vegetables and fruits are not always available. Scarcity of water and limited availability of fresh vegetables have had their effect on the cuisine of Rajasthan. Food has also been affected by the war like lifestyle of the Rajputs. Food that can last several days and can be had without heating is preferred. Lentils, millets and barley snacks, such as Bikaneri Bhujia, dairy and ghee characterize the food of the region.

Rajputs have been avid hunters. And their diet, inter alia, comprises Laal Maas, Safed Maas, khargosh (rabbit) and of course partridges and quails. I remember, my husband often bought quails at Kotputli, on the highway, on his return journey from Jaipur which I would then cook in red chillies. The hunt for partridges is now banned.

The recipes that follow in this section are typically Rajasthani Panchmel Dal and Dal Baati Churma, a crowning glory of Rajasthani dish, served during all festive occasions.

LENTILS IN COCONUT MILK

PREPARATION TIME
30 minutes

COOKING TIME
30 minutes

SERVES
6–8

- 200 g red lentils (masoor dal)
- ¾th coconut
- 65 ml oil
- 4 onions, finely sliced
- ⅓rd tsp turmeric powder ⎫
- 4–5 dry whole red chillies ⎬ ground to a paste
- 6–7 cloves of garlic ⎪
- 1 tsp cumin seeds ⎭
- 10–15 curry leaves
- 1 tsp sugar
- Juice of 1–2 limes
- Salt

Gently spiced and enriched with coconut milk, this is a simple Parsi dal.

Wash and soak the lentils in water for 30 minutes. Drain the water.

Grate the coconut and add one glass of water. Churn it in a mixie. Sieve to extract coconut milk. Set it aside.

Heat the oil and fry the onions till they turn golden brown. Keep half aside to be used later.

Add the ground paste specified in the ingredients to the onions. Stir fry for a minute. Sprinkle a little water, then add salt and drained lentils. Mix and stir fry for 2–3 minutes. Add 3 glasses of water and cook on a high flame till the lentils come to a boil and then on medium-low flame till tender. Mash lightly.

Add the coconut milk. Mix and cook further for 4–5 minutes. Add curry leaves, sugar and lime juice.

Serve hot, with a garnish of fried onions.

KATACHI AMTI

PREPARATION TIME
10–15 minutes

COOKING TIME
25–30 minutes

SERVES
6

An enticing Maharashtrian dal, mildly sweet and sour because of the use of tamarind and jaggery. Goes well with both steaming hot rice and roti.

. . . .

- 200 g red lentils (masoor dal)
- 2 tbsp Bengal gram lentils, split and skinned (chana dal)
- 2 tbsp red gram lentils (arhar dal)
- 50 g tamarind
- 2 tbsp ghee
- 1 tsp mustard seeds
- 1 tsp cumin seeds
- 3–4 cloves
- 1 inch cinnamon stick
- A pinch of asafoetida
- 2–3 green chillies, slit
- 1½ tbsp jaggery
- A few sprigs of fresh green coriander, chopped
- Salt

Wash and soak the lentils in 4 glasses of water for 30 minutes. Drain the water once the lentils are done soaking.

In a heavy base pan, boil the lentils in 3½ glasses of water till tender. Mash and sieve. Set it aside.

Wash and soak the tamarind in one cup of warm water for about 15 minutes. Mash and sieve to extract tamarind juice. Set aside.

In a separate heavy-base pan, heat the ghee. Add mustard seeds followed after 5 seconds by cumin seeds. When the mustard starts to crackle and the cumin seeds turn light brown, add cloves and cinnamon, immediately followed by asafoetida. Add the previously cooked lentils, tamarind juice, green chillies, jaggery and salt. Let the lentils come to a boil. Cook for 5 minutes. Turn off the heat. The dish has medium-thin consistency.

Serve hot, garnished with fresh green coriander.

MOONG USAL

PREPARATION TIME
15 minutes

COOKING TIME
30 minutes

SERVES
6

This dal is nutritious, healthy and rich in fibre. Typically Maharashtrian recipe, where moth beans are flavoured with jaggery, peanuts and coconut.

- 200 g moth beans (moth)
- ½ tsp turmeric powder
- 55 ml oil
- 1 tsp mustard seeds
- A pinch of asafoetida
- 2–3 medium onions, chopped
- 2 tomatoes, chopped
- 1 tsp red chilli powder
- ½ tsp garam masala
- 1 tbsp jaggery
- 1 tbsp roasted and crushed peanuts
- 1 tbsp desiccated coconut, finely grated
- A few sprigs of fresh green coriander, chopped
- Salt

Wash and soak the lentils in water overnight. The water should be about 3 inches above the level of the lentils. Drain the water and wash the lentils before cooking.

Transfer the lentils to a pressure cooker. Add salt, turmeric powder and 2½ glasses of water. Cook till 1–2 whistles. Then turn off the heat. Allow the dal to cool. Uncover and boil away excess water. The lentils should be about 80 per cent cooked.

Heat the oil in a heavy pan. Add mustard seeds. When mustard starts to crackle, add asafoetida followed immediately by onions. Fry the onions till they become translucent. Add tomatoes and red chilli powder. Cook till the oil starts to separate. Add the previously boiled lentils, garam masala and sprinkle a little water. Mix and cook covered on a medium flame for about 10 minutes or till the lentils are tender.

Add jaggery, peanuts and coconut. Mix and cook covered for another 4–5 minutes.

Serve hot garnished with fresh green coriander. This is a somewhat semi-dry dish.

MOONG SPROUT

PREPARATION TIME
5 minutes

COOKING TIME
10–15 minutes

SERVES
4–6

- 200 g green gram lentils, whole and sprouted (moong dal, sabut and sprouted)
- 1½ tbsp oil
- 1 onion, cut horizontally in the middle and then sliced
- 2 medium tomatoes, chopped
- 3 green chillies, slit down the middle
- A few sprigs of fresh green coriander, chopped
- Salt

Sprouted lentils are extremely nutritious. This one too is invitingly simple, light and nourishing. A fine example of how a few ingredients can make a marvellous dish.

Heat the oil in a heavy-base pan. Add the onion and, after just 1–2 minutes, add the tomatoes, 2 green chillies, half of the fresh coriander and salt. Add the sprouts. Mix and cook for 2–3 minutes covered. Add about ¾th glass of warm water. Cook covered, first on high flame and then low flame for 4–5 minutes till the sprouts are a little soft. Do not overcook. The sprouts should be just about tender. When done, there should be just a little water left in the dish to keep it juicy and not dry. Also add the remaining green chillies and the coriander. Mix. Turn off the flame.

Serve hot as a side dish. Works as a substitute for salad too.

HOW TO MAKE BEAN SPROUTS Wash and soak 300 g green lentils in 4 glasses of water over night. Next day drain the water.

Take a largish coarse cotton cloth and make it moist in water. Place the lentils in the centre, somewhat flattened and cover them from the sides. Now place that in a bowl and cover it with a lid.

The lentils will sprout in 2–4 days depending on the weather. In winter, lentils take longer to sprout. Sprinkle a little water over the cloth while the lentils are sprouting, to keep it moist.

Use the sprouts as per your requirement. The balance can be kept in the fridge in a suitable dish for use later.

AMTI

PREPARATION TIME
15 minutes

COOKING TIME
30 minutes

SERVES
6

- 300 g chickpeas (Kabuli chana)
- 2 onions, sliced
- 2 tbsp desiccated coconut, grated
- 1 tbsp poppy seeds
- 3 dry whole red chillies
- A few sprigs of fresh green coriander
- 1 tsp pepper powder or red chilli powder
- 1/3rd tsp turmeric powder
- 1/2 tsp garam masala
- 65 ml oil
- 1 tsp ginger paste
- 1 tsp garlic paste
- Salt

Amti is a Maharashtrian dal made from chickpeas. Chickpeas are versatile and go well with all sorts of ingredients. The earthy flavour of the chickpeas, along with the mild sweetness of coconut and poppy seeds, is enhanced by the use of red chillies, pepper and garam masala.

Wash and soak the chickpeas in 4–5 glasses of water overnight. Next morning, drain the water and wash the chickpeas afresh. Pressure cook in 3½–4 glasses of water. After 2–3 whistles, lower the flame and cook for another 5–8 minutes. Open when the pressure subsides. The lentils at this stage should be tender. Mash lightly.

Heat a heavy-base pan and dry roast the onions till they turn deep brown. Remove and set aside. Then dry roast the coconut, poppy seeds and the dry red chillies. Grind all this and the browned onions along with the fresh coriander in a mixie to a fine paste. Add salt, pepper or red chilli powder, turmeric powder and garam masala to this paste.

Heat the oil. Add ginger and garlic paste. When the paste turns golden, add the ground masala and fry for 2–3 minutes. Then add to the previously cooked lentils and cook for 6–7 minutes.

Serve hot.

ARHAR DAL WITH METHI

PREPARATION TIME
20 minutes

COOKING TIME
25 minutes

SERVES
6

- 200 g red gram lentils (arhar dal)
- 1½ cup freshly plucked leaves of fresh green fenugreek
- ⅓rd tsp turmeric
- 1 tsp red chilli powder
- A pinch of asafoetida
- 1 tsp jaggery
- 4 kokums (alternatively, ⅓rd cup tamarind juice)
- 2 cloves
- ½ inch cinnamon stick
- ¼th cup desiccated coconut, grated
- ½ tsp cumin seeds
- 1 tsp coriander seeds
- Salt

} dry roasted lightly and powdered

BAGHAR
- 3 tbsp oil
- 1 tsp mustard seeds
- ½ tsp fenugreek seeds
- A few curry leaves

A Maharashtrian dal, gently sweet and sour with a fascinating combination of taste and colour. Dry roasted and powdered spices give this dish an amazing lift.

Wash and soak the lentils in water for 20 minutes. Drain the water.

Add 3 glasses of water and bring the lentils to a boil. Cook first on high and then on medium-low flame till the lentils are half done.

At this stage, add all the ingredients to the dal except the baghar ingredients.

Bring the dal to a boil. Reduce heat and simmer for about 10–15 minutes till the lentils and fenugreek are tender and well blended.

For the baghar, heat the oil in a pan. Add mustard seeds. When they start to pop, add fenugreek seeds and after just about 5 seconds add the curry leaves. After a few seconds, pour the baghar over the lentils and mix.

The dish has medium consistency. Serve hot.

PURANPOLI

PREPARATION TIME
10 minutes

COOKING TIME
45–50 minutes

SERVES
6–8

PURAN
- 250 g Bengal gram lentils, split and skinned (chana dal)
- 200 g jaggery
- 8 cardamom pods, powdered
- ¼th tsp nutmeg powder
- A few strands of saffron

POLI
- 175 g wheat flour (atta)
- 2 tbsp refined flour (maida)
- 2 tbsp oil
- 3 tbsp ghee
- ⅓rd tsp salt

Puranpoli is a traditional Maharashtrian bread with sweet, lentil filling. 'Puran' is stuffing and 'poli' is the outer covering. Puranpoli is made on festive occasions such as Ganesh Chaturthi, Raksha Bandhan, Diwali and Holi. It can be served as a dessert or part of a meal. It is particularly popular in Gujarat also.

Wash and soak the lentils in 3–4 glasses of water for 30 minutes. Drain the water.

Transfer the lentils to a pressure cooker. Add 1½ glasses of water and cook on high flame till 2–3 whistles. Reduce the flame to medium–low and cook further for 6–8 minutes. Turn off the flame. Once the pressure subsides, open the pressure cooker.

Now crush the jaggery and add it to the lentils along with the cardamom, nutmeg powder and saffron. Cook till the jaggery melts and the lentils becomes thick. Set aside.

Separately, prepare the dough for poli. Mix the wheat flour, refined flour, 2 tbsp oil and salt. Adding a little water, knead to make soft dough.

Divide the dough and lentils into 8 equal portions. Take one portion of the dough and roll it in your palms to make a ball. Brushing lightly with oil, roll it out to a diameter of about 4 inches. Place one portion of the lentils in the centre. Lift from all sides, fold the dough towards the centre and seal in the middle. Roll it once again to a diameter of 6 inches, applying a little oil to the surface.

Heat a griddle and place the rolled disc on it. Turn it over after 1–2 minutes. When the bread is golden on both sides and has some gold–brown spots, apply 1–2 tsp ghee on each side before turning the bread over. Cook till both sides are golden brown. Repeat the process for the remaining ingredients.

Serve hot after applying a little ghee on top.

GOA

GOAN DAL MASALA

PREPARATION TIME
15 minutes

COOKING TIME
30–40 minutes

SERVES
6–8

With its blue-green sea, silvery beaches and tall coconut palms, Goa has irresistible charm. Rice, sea food, coconut, vegetables, meat, pork and local spices are some of the main ingredients of Goan cuisine.

During one of our visits to the state, we stayed at a beach resort called 360. (This was when I was researching for my earlier book Biryani.) Roland Monteiro, a chef in that resort, graciously shared this recipe of Goan Dal Masala and many more with me. A simple dish yet typically very Goan, where spices and coconut are used to the best advantage.

- 250 g red gram lentils (arhar dal)
- ⅓rd tsp turmeric powder
- 3 tbsp oil
- ⅓rd fresh coconut, grated
- 3 medium onions, sliced
- 4–5 dry red chillies, whole
- 2 tbsp coriander seeds
- 6–7 cloves
- 10 peppercorns
- 1 tsp cumin seeds
- Salt

} X

BAGHAR
- 2 tbsp oil
- 1 tsp flat mustard seeds
- A few curry leaves

Wash and soak the lentils for about 20–30 minutes. The water should be 2–3 inches above the surface of lentils. Drain the water.

Place the lentils in a pressure cooker along with salt, turmeric and 3–3½ glasses of water. Pressure cook on high flame till 1–2 whistles. When the pressure subsides, open the pressure cooker and check if the lentils are tender. If required, cook further without the lid till tender.

In a pan, heat 3 tbsp oil and sauté the coconut and onions for 3–4 minutes. Remove from the heat and grind together the coconut and onions along with the spices at 'X' till you have a fine paste.

Now heat 2 tbsp oil Add mustard seeds. When they start to splutter, add curry leaves. After about 5–10 seconds, add the ground masala and fry for 2–3 minutes.
Add this baghar to the lentils, mix and cook further for 5–6 minutes.

This dish has medium consistency. Goes well with rice or bread.

Serve hot.

COCONUT AND CHILLI LENTILS

PREPARATION TIME
15–20 minutes

COOKING TIME
40 minutes

SERVES
6–8

- 75 g green gram lentils (moong dal, sabut)
- 75 g red gram lentils (arhar dal)
- ½ tsp turmeric powder
- 1 tsp red chilli powder
- ¼th tsp asafoetida
- ¼th fresh coconut, ground
- ½ cup coconut milk
- ¾th cup shallots, finely sliced into rings
- 3 green chillies, slit
- 10–15 curry leaves
- 1 tsp coconut oil
- Salt

Coconut, shallots, red chillies and curry leaves together bring out the magnificence of this Goan dish.

Wash and soak the green gram lentils in 2 glasses of water overnight. Next morning wash and soak the red gram lentils in 2 glasses of water for 1 hour. Drain the water just before cooking.

Now place the lentils in a heavy-base pan. Add 2 glasses of water. Cook first on high flame to bring the lentils to a boil. Then reduce heat to medium, and cook covered till the lentils are tender and kind of dry.

Mix turmeric powder, red chilli powder and asafoetida in a little water. Add the mixture to the lentils. Also add salt, ground coconut, coconut milk and shallots. Add 1–1½ glasses of warm water. Cook on medium flame till the shallots are tender.

Add the slit green chillies. Crush the curry leaves and mix with coconut oil. Add to the lentils.

For the baghar, heat the vegetable and coconut oil together. Fry all the baghar ingredients for 1–2 minutes. Pour the baghar over the lentils. Mix.

This dish has medium-thick consistency.

Serve hot.

COCONUT AND CHILLY LENTILS

KHICHRA

PREPARATION TIME
20 minutes

COOKING TIME
45 minutes

SERVES
8–10

An amazing mix of lentils, meat and spices, this Muslim dish is a variation of Haleem. A wholesome and delectable dish, it is popular in western India, and transforms the traditional dish known as Khichra.

- 50 g Bengal gram lentils, split and skinned (chana dal)
- 50 g black gram lentils, split and skinned (urad dal, dhuli)
- 50 g red lentils (masoor dal)
- 50 g black-eyed beans (lobia)
- 50 g broken wheat (dalia)
- 220 ml oil
- 6 large onions, sliced
- 1 tbsp ginger, chopped
- 1 tbsp crushed garlic
- ½ tsp turmeric powder
- 1 tsp red chilli powder
- 2 1-inch stick cinnamon
- 3–4 green cardamom pods
- 4 cloves
- 1 tsp coriander powder
- 1 tsp cumin powder
- 5–6 green chillies, chopped
- ⅓rd cup fresh green coriander, chopped
- 1 kg boneless meat, cut into medium-sized pieces
- 150 g yoghurt, whisked
- 1 tbsp ghee
- Salt

GARNISH
- Fried onions
- 2 green chillies, chopped
- A few mint leaves, chopped
- 1 tbsp julienned ginger
- 2 lemons, sliced

Wash and soak the lentils, including the broken wheat in water, making sure the level is well above the surface of the lentils. Soak for about 1 hour. Drain the water.

Pressure cook the lentils with 4–5 glasses of water and a little salt till 3 whistles. Once the pressure subsides, open the lid. The lentils should be tender.

Heat the oil in another pressure cooker. Fry the onions till golden brown. Remove half of the fried onions and set aside for the garnish. Leave about 110 ml oil in the pan and continue cooking. Add ginger and garlic. After a minute or so, add all the spices i.e., turmeric, red chilli powder, cinnamon, cardamom, cloves, coriander and cumin powder.

Next, add the green chillies, fresh green coriander and salt. Now add the meat, mix and fry for about 5 minutes. Add the whisked yoghurt and fry it further for 6–7 minutes till the oil starts to separate. Add 3 glasses of water and pressure cook till 3 whistles. Reduce the flame to low and let the meat simmer for another about 7–8 minutes. Turn off the heat. After the pressure subsides, open the lid.

Transfer the meat to a large heavy-base pan (karahi is the best option). Also add the previously cooked lentils and the ghee. Mix and cook on medium-low flame till well blended. The dish has porridge-like consistency.

Serve hot, decorated with all garnish ingredients including the reserved fried onions.

PARSI MASOOR DAL

PREPARATION TIME
20 minutes

COOKING TIME
30–40 minutes

SERVES
6–8

- 200 g ochre lentils (masoor dal, sabut)
- 1 onion, halved
- 1 brinjal (round variety weighing about 150 g) cut into 4 pieces
- 82 ml oil
- 3 onions, finely sliced
- 1 inch ginger piece
- 5–6 garlic cloves
- 3 dry red chillies
- 1 tsp cumin seeds
- 1 tsp coriander seeds } ground to a paste
- 1 green cardamom
- 3–4 cloves
- 1 tsp peppercorns
- 1 tsp vinegar
- 1 tsp sugar
- Salt

A flavourful Parsi dish made with assertive use of spices and pepped-up with pepper, vinegar and sugar.

Wash and soak the lentils in water for 1 hour. Drain the water.

Place the lentils in a heavy-base pan. Add 2½ glasses of water, onion and brinjal. Cook first on a high flame till the lentils come to a boil. Lower flame and cook covered till the lentils are tender and the water absorbed. Do not allow the lentils to get mushy. When done, the lentils should be tender and yet remain whole.

Carefully lift the brinjal and the onion pieces and pass through a sieve. Keep aside.

Heat the oil. Fry the onions till golden brown. Remove half and set it aside. Add the ground spices and salt to the remaining onion. Mix and fry for about 2 minutes. Add the sieved onion and brinjal. Mix and fry further for 3–4 minutes.

Add the previously boiled lentils to the fried masala. Also add vinegar and sugar. Mix gently.

Serve hot, garnished with the reserved fried onions.

ANGOOR KI DAL

PREPARATION TIME
10 minutes

COOKING TIME
30 minutes

SERVES
6

- 200 g red gram lentils (arhar dal)
- ⅓rd tsp turmeric
- 2 tbsp ghee
- 1 tsp mustard seeds
- 1 tsp cumin seeds
- 1 tsp red chilli powder
- 1 tsp sugar
- 1 cup ripe green grapes
- Salt

This dish from Gujarat, which gets its unique flavour from fresh green grapes and is a fine example of how just a few ingredients can make a marvellous dish.

. . . .

Wash and soak the lentils well covered in water for about 20 minutes. Drain the water.

Pressure cook the lentils in 2¼ glasses of water with salt and turmeric. After 1–2 whistles, turn off the flame. When the pressure subsides, open the lid. The lentils should be tender but not mushy. If not, cook further without pressure till tender.

Heat the ghee in a pan. Add mustard seeds. When the mustard starts to splutter, add cumin seeds. When the cumin turns brown, turn off the flame. After 5 seconds, add the red chilli powder and then add the baghar to the already cooked lentils. Also add sugar and grapes. Mix and cook for 2 minutes.

When done, the lentils should have medium-thick consistency and should not be watery.

Serve hot.

DHANSAK

PREPARATION TIME
30 minutes

COOKING TIME
30–40 minutes

SERVES
6–8

To quote the noted columnist Vir Sanghvi, 'It is the greatest dal and meat dish ever invented anywhere in the world.' A classic dish that comes from Parsi cuisine, it is regarded as the king of all dal-meat dishes.

The vegetarian version of Dhansak is equally popular. This dish is made with lentils and vegetables where flavours are enhanced by inclusion of herbs and spices, ghee and lime juice.

Dhansak is traditionally served with plain or caramelized brown rice.

- 100 g red gram lentils (arhar dal)
- 50 g red lentils (masoor dal)
- 100 g red pumpkin, cut into medium-sized pieces
- ½ cup plucked fresh fenugreek leaves   } A
- 2 brinjals, cut into small pieces
- 2 tomatoes, chopped
- ½ tsp turmeric powder
- 55 ml oil
- 2 onions, sliced fine
- 6–8 cloves of garlic
- 1½ inch ginger piece
- 1½ tsp cumin seeds
- 2 tsp coriander seeds   } B — ground to paste
- 4–6 dry whole red chillies
- 1 tbsp vinegar
- 1 tbsp ghee
- Juice of 1 lime
- Salt

Wash the lentils and soak in liberal quantity of water for about 20–30 minutes. Drain the water.

Place the lentils in a heavy-base pan. Add about 3 glasses of water and salt, and all the ingredients at 'A'. Cover the pan and cook on a high flame till the dish comes to a boil. Reduce the flame to medium-low flame and cook till the lentils are tender. Mash and sieve.

Heat oil in a heavy-base pan. Fry the onions till they are light brown. Add the paste at 'B' and fry till it turns light brown. Add the lentils. Once the lentils are cooked, simmer on low flame for about 10 minutes. Add ghee and lime juice.

The dish has medium-thick consistency.

Serve hot

GUJARATI MOONG DAL

PREPARATION TIME
10 minutes

COOKING TIME
30 minutes

SERVES
6

This dal will have you in raptures. It has a light and soupy texture with refreshing blend of ginger, green chillies and fresh green coriander.

The combination of tamarind and jaggery lend it a mouth-watering sweet and sour flavour. An absolute favourite of my daughters, Gauri and Nainika.

- 200 g green gram lentils (moong dal, sabut)
- ⅓rd tsp turmeric powder
- 2 tbsp oil
- 1 tsp cumin seeds
- A pinch of asafoetida
- 1½ tbsp ginger, sliced
- 4–5 green chillies, slit down the middle
- ⅓rd tea cup, fresh green coriander, chopped
- 60 g tamarind (soak in ¾th glass of warm water for 10–15 minutes. Mash and extract tamarind juice)
- 60 g jaggery
- Salt

Wash and soak the lentils in 4 glasses of water for 30 minutes. Drain the water.

Place the lentils in a pressure cooker. Add 4 glasses of water, salt and turmeric powder. Pressure cook till 1 whistle. Turn off the flame. Open the when the pressure subsides. The lentils should be tender at this stage. If not cook further with lid on till the lentils are tender.

Now take a heavy-bottom pan. Heat the oil. Add cumin seeds. When the cumin seeds turn golden, add a pinch of asafoetida. Then add half of ginger, 2–3 green chillies and half of the fresh green coriander. Add the previously cooked green lentils. Bring the dish to boil. Add tamarind juice and jaggery. Cook for 5 minutes. Add the remaining ginger, green chillies and coriander. Cook for just another minute and turn the flame off.

This dal has medium-thin consistency.

Serve hot with steaming hot rice.

MOOGER DAL

PREPARATION TIME
5 minutes

COOKING TIME
20 minutes

SERVES
6–8

- 250 g green gram lentils, split and skinned (moong dal, dhuli)
- 2 tbsp ghee
- 4–5 cloves
- 15–20 curry leaves
- ¼th tsp turmeric
- ¾th tsp red chilli powder
- A few sprigs of fresh green coriander, chopped
- A few lemon wedges
- Salt

A breeze to make, Mooger Dal is a simple and delicious dal from Rajasthan. Ghee and cloves work their magic in this dish, and the combination of green coriander and lemon wedges infuse it with fresh flavours.

. . . .

Wash and soak the lentils in 4 glasses of water for 30 minutes, and then drain the water.

Heat ghee in a heavy-base pan. Add cloves followed in a few seconds by the curry leaves. After just a few seconds add the lentils. Also add salt, turmeric and red chilli powder. Mix. Stir and sauté for 1–2 minutes. Add 2½ glasses of water and let the dish come to a boil.

Lower the heat and cook covered till the lentils are tender and the water absorbed. The lentils should not get mushy. Each grain, though tender, must remain separate, with only some moisture left.

Serve hot, garnished with fresh coriander leaves and wedges of lemon.

PANCHMEL DAL

PREPARATION TIME
15 minutes

COOKING TIME
30 minutes

SERVES
6–8

- 50 g green gram lentils, split and skinned (moong dal, dhuli)
- 50 g green gram lentils, whole (moong dal, sabut)
- 50 g black gram lentils, split and skinned (urad dal, dhuli)
- 50 g red gram lentils (arhar dal)
- 50 g Bengal gram lentils, split and skinned (chana dal)
- ½ tsp turmeric powder
- ½ tsp dry ginger powder (sonth)
- 2 green chillies slit
- 1 tbsp jaggery
- Salt

BAGHAR
- 3 tbsp ghee
- 1 tsp cumin seeds
- 3–4 cloves
- 1 black cardamom
- 2 bay leaves
- 15–20 curry leaves
- A pinch of asafoetida
- 1 tsp red chilli powder
- 1 tomato, skinned and chopped

A popular dal from Rajasthan. As the name suggests, this is a combination of five lentils. Dry ginger powder, jaggery and the rich seasoning with ghee, all result in an extravagant dish.

· ·

Wash all the lentils together and soak them in 3 -4 glasses of water for 30 minutes. Drain the water.

Transfer the lentils to a heavy-bottom pan. Add 3½ glasses of water, salt, turmeric and ginger powder. Cook the lentils till tender. Add the green chillies and the jaggery.

In a separate pan, heat ghee. Add the cumin seeds. When the cumin starts to turn golden, add cloves, black cardamom and bay leaves, followed by curry leaves asafoetida, red chilli powder and then the tomato. As soon as the tomato gets soft, add the baghar to the lentils, mix and cover.

Serve hot.

DAL BAATI CHURMA

PREPARATION TIME
20 minutes

COOKING TIME
1 hour 30 minutes

SERVES
8

Dal Baati Churma is a traditional Rajasthani treat made on all festive and special occasions. It holds the pride of place in Rajasthani cuisine

A complete meal in itself, it consists of Panchmel Dal—the name derived from a mix of five lentils cooked together. Baaties, which are flaky round patties baked or deep fried and Churma, which is a sweet desert. Liberal use of ghee makes it rich, delicious and truly heart-warming.

DAL

- 50 g Bengal gram lentils, split and skinned (chana dal)
- 50 g black gram lentils, split and skinned (urad dal, dhuli)
- 50 g green gram lentils, whole (moong dal, sabut)
- 50 g red gram lentils (arhar dal)
- ⅓rd tsp turmeric
- 1½ tsp red chilli powder
- 1 tsp coriander powder
- ½ tsp garam masala
- A few sprigs of fresh green coriander, chopped
- 1–2 tbsp ghee to drizzle over the lentils while serving
- Salt

TO MAKE DAL Wash the lentils well and soak them in 3–4 glasses of water. Then drain the water.

Pressure cook the lentils with salt, turmeric, red chilli powder and coriander powder in 3 glasses of water till 2–3 whistles. Open when the pressure subsides. Add garam masala and mix.

Mash to give it a thick-soup-like consistency. Also add the chopped coriander.

For the baghar, heat the ghee. Add all the ingredients at 'A'. Saute for a few seconds and add the baghar to the already cooked lentils. Mix and cover.

TO MAKE BAATI To make Baaties, mix wheat flour, semolina, gram flour, milk, fennel seeds, carom seeds and salt together. Knead to make stiff dough.

Divide the dough into 10 equal portions. Take one portion in your fist and roll it into a small ball. Flatten it slightly. Press it in the middle with your thumb to make an indentation. Repeat the process for the remaining Baaties.

Bake them in a pre-heated oven at 180°C for 20–25 minutes. Else, deep fry them on medium-low flame till golden brown. When ready, brush them with ghee.

BAGHAR

- 2 tbsp ghee
- 3 cloves
- 1 bay leaf
- 1 tsp cumin seeds
- ½ tsp grated ginger
- 2 green chillies, split
- A pinch of asafoetida

A

BAATI

- 150 g whole wheat flour (atta)
- 75 g semolina
- 2 tbsp gram flour
- ½ cup milk
- 1 tsp fennel seeds
- ¼th tsp carom seeds
- Salt
- Oil for deep drying
- 2–3 tbsp ghee for brushing the Baaties

CHURMA

- 100 g whole wheat flour (atta)
- 50 g semolina (suji)
- 4 tbsp ghee
- Ghee for frying
- 8–10 almonds, slivered
- Seeds of 6–7 cardamom pods, powdered
- 4 tbsp powdered sugar

TO MAKE CHURMA Mix whole wheat flour, semolina and ghee and add about ¼th cup water. Knead to make stiff dough.

Divide the dough into 8 equal portions. Take each portion and shape it like a Baati with an indentation at the centre.

Now heat the ghee. Fry the Baaties, a few at a time on medium-low flame till rich golden brown. Place on an absorbent paper. When cool, crush them with hands and blend in a mixer to a coarse powder. Add almonds, cardamom and powdered sugar, and mix.

To serve, heat the lentils. Place the Baaties in a serving dish. Pour the dal over these and drizzle ghee over the lentils. Serve with Churma on the side.

DAL BAATI CHURMA

Neighbouring Countries

SINDHI DAL CURRY

PREPARATION TIME
30 minutes

COOKING TIME
30 minutes

SERVES
8

This dal is originally from Sindh, which is now a part of Pakistan. A host of vegetables are used in this dish and some of our Sindhi friends make it with just gypsy beans. Flavours of the different vegetables, combined with the roasted gram flour and tamarind makes this a real treat. It is our favourite for Sunday lunch and is normally accompanied with papad and a dish of fried potatoes called Took in Sindhi.

. . . .

- 200 g red gram lentils (arhar dal)
- 50 g gram flour
- 75 g tamarind
- 100 g gypsy beans (gawar phalli)
- 1 potato
- 1 large tomato
- 2 brinjals
- 1 radish
- 6–8 okras
- 50 g cauliflower
- 2 green chillies
- 1 large onion

A

- 55 ml oil
- 1 tsp cumin seeds
- ½ tsp fenugreek seeds
- 3–4 dry whole red chillies
- ½ tsp turmeric powder
- 1 tsp red chilli powder
- A few sprigs of fresh green coriander, chopped
- Salt

Wash the lentils and then soak for 30 minutes. Drain them and then boil in 3–3½ glasses of water till tender. Lightly mash and set aside.

Lightly dry roast the gram flour till it turns a rich gold colour and there is a lovely aroma. Do not over brown. Add 1½ glasses of water to it and mix well. Set aside.

Wash and soak the tamarind in 1 cup of warm water for 10–15 minutes. Mash and sieve the mixture to get tamarind juice. Set aside.

Slice off the sides of the gypsy beans to take the strings off and cut all the vegetables into medium–large sized pieces. Keep the okra whole, chopping just the stem off.

Heat the oil. Add cumin seeds and then fenugreek seeds and dry red whole chillies. When the chillies darken, add all the vegetables at 'A'. Also add salt, turmeric and red chilli powder. Mix and cook for about

Continued. . .

10 minutes. Add the boiled lentils, gram flour water and tamarind juice. Cook till the vegetable are tender and contents well blended. Turn off the heat and add fresh chopped coriander. The dish should have medium-thin consistency.

Serve hot along with plain rice, papad and Took (Took is potatoes cut into medium-thick slices and deep fried golden brown with sprinkling of salt and red chilli powder).

BHUGAL

PREPARATION TIME
10 minutes

COOKING TIME
30 minutes

SERVES
6–8

- 200 g Bengal gram lentils, split and skinned (chana dal)
- 55 ml oil
- 3 medium onions, chopped
- 1 inch ginger piece, chopped
- 3 green chillies
- 2 medium tomatoes, chopped
- 1 tsp red chilli powder
- 2 bay leaves
- 1 black cardamom, cracked opened slightly
- 1 inch cinnamon stick
- ½ tsp garam masala
- A few sprigs of fresh green coriander, chopped
- Salt

A delicious Sindhi dal and a breeze to make.

Wash the lentils and soak in 3 glasses of water for 30 minutes. Drain the water just before cooking.

Heat the oil in a pressure cooker. Add onions and fry till they are dark pink. Add ginger and green chillies. After a few seconds add the chopped tomatoes, and also salt and red chilli powder. Stir and fry for 2–3 minutes and then add bay leaves, black cardamom and cinnamon. Add the drained lentils and fry first on high flame and then low for about 5 minutes.

When the oil starts to surface, add 2½ glasses of water. Pressure cook on a high flame till 1 whistle. Then reduce flame to low and cook for about 4–5 minutes till the lentils are tender.

Transfer hot to a dish. Sprinkle garam masala and garnish with fresh green coriander.

TIDALI

PREPARATION TIME
10 minutes

COOKING TIME
25 minutes

SERVES
6–8

- 75 g black gram lentils, whole (urad dal, sabut)
- 75 g green gram lentils, whole (moong dal, sabut)
- 50 g Bengal gram lentils, split and skinned (chana dal)
- ⅓rd tsp turmeric powder
- 1 inch piece ginger, chopped
- 4–5 cloves of garlic, crushed
- 2–3 green chillies
- 4 cloves
- Salt

A

BAGHAR
- 2 tbsp ghee
- 6–7 cloves of garlic, chopped
- ½ tsp red chilli powder
- Juice of 1 lime
- A few sprigs of fresh green coriander, chopped

A Sindhi dal made with a combination of three different tasty dals and hence the name Tidali. Ghee used in the baghar makes this delicious. The juice of lime and fresh coriander further perk up its flavour.

Wash all the lentils together and soak them in 3 glasses of water for 30 minutes. Drain the water.

Place the lentils in a pressure cooker along with salt and all the ingredients at 'A' and 2 glasses of water. Pressure cook on high flame. After 1 whistle, turn off the flame. Uncover when the pressure subsides. Check to see if the lentils are tender. If not, cook further partly covered and add a little water if necessary. When done, the lentils should be tender, yet individual grains visible with just a hint of moisture.

Heat the lentils just before serving and transfer them to a serving dish.

Heat the ghee in a separate pan. Add garlic. When the garlic turns golden brown, add red chilli powder and immediately pour the baghar over the dish. Add the lime juice over the dish and garnish with fresh green coriander.

SAWA SAG WITH 2 DALS

PREPARATION TIME
20 minutes

COOKING TIME
30 minutes

SERVES
6–8

This is a Sindhi dish in which the lentils are cooked with fresh green spinach and other vegetables. The result is a rich and delicious intermingling of flavours. The tempering with ghee, gram flour and red chillies infuses the dish with extra flavour.

- 750 g spinach, washed and cut along with only the tender stems
- 50 g Bengal gram lentils, split and skinned (chana dal)
- 50 g green gram lentils, split and skinned (moong dal, dhuli)
- 1 onion, roughly chopped
- 1 cup green gourd or turnip, skinned and chopped
- 1 potato, skinned and chopped
- 1 tomato chopped
- 1½ tsp ginger, chopped
- 6–7 cloves of garlic, chopped
- 2–3 green chillies

X

BAGHAR
- 4 tbsp ghee
- 1 tbsp gram flour
- 1 tsp red chilli powder
- Salt

Place the spinach along with all the ingredients at 'X', salt and 1 glass of water in a pressure cooker. Cook till 1–2 whistles. Reduce the flame and cook for another 5 minutes. Turn off the flame. Open when the pressure subsides. The lentils and vegetables at this stage should be tender.

Heat ghee in a pan. Add the gram flour to it and sauté till it turns golden brown and starts to emit a nice aroma. Turn off the flame. Add red chilli powder and mix.

Now pour this gram flour and red chilli powder baghar into the dish. Mix and mash the ingredients. Cook further for 6–7 minutes. The dish should have medium–thick, porridge-like consistency.

Serve hot.

SRI LANKAN COCONUT LENTILS

PREPARATION TIME
10 minutes

COOKING TIME
25 minutes

SERVES
6

It was during a trip to Sri Lanka to bring in the New Year that my family and I made a halt at Galle. We stayed at a most beautiful beach villa called 'INDISCH', where we had the entire villa and its full staff at our disposal. We were fortunate to be treated to meal after meal of Sri Lankan delicacies and fresh coconut water, straight from the coconut trees in the garden of the villa. It was there that I learnt this recipe from a young enthusiastic chef.

Coconut and spices feature regularly in many Sri Lankan dishes as they grow in abundance in the region. Coconut lends this dish a mild sweetness while helping to amalgamate the flavours. Shallots and curry leaves of course provide added flavour.

- 200 g red lentils (masoor dal)
- ¾th fresh coconut
- 2 tbsp sliced shallots
- 3–4 cloves of garlic, crushed
- 3 green chillies, chopped
- ⅓rd cup fresh curry leaves
- ⅓rd tsp turmeric powder
- 1 tsp cumin and black pepper powder
- ½ tsp fenugreek seeds
- Juice of 1 lime
- Salt

} A

BAGHAR
- 3 tbsp oil
- 15–20 curry leaves
- 3–4 dry red chillies
- 1 tbsp finely sliced shallot

Wash and soak the lentils for 30 minutes.
Drain the water.

Grate 3/4th of a fresh coconut. Add 1 glass of warm water and churn the mixture in a blender. Squeeze the coconut by hand to extract coconut milk. Set aside.

Put the lentils in a pressure cooker along with salt, all the ingredients at 'A' and 3 glasses of water. Pressure cook till 1 whistle. Remove from the flame. Allow the pressure to subside and then open the lid. If necessary, cook further without pressure till the lentils are tender. Mash the lentils lightly. Add coconut milk and mix.

For the baghar, heat the oil. Add curry leaves and after about 5–7 seconds, add the red chillies. When the curry leaves become crisp and the red chillies turn reddish brown, add the sliced shallot. Fry till golden brown. Pour the baghar over the lentils. Mix. Add the lime juice.

Serve hot.

SRI LANKAN PARIPPU HODI

PREPARATION TIME
10–15 minutes

COOKING TIME
25 minutes

SERVES
8

- 250 g red lentils
- (masoor dal)
- ¼th tsp turmeric powder
- ½ tsp red chilli powder
- 1 heaped tsp Sri Lankan curry powder
- 1 inch cinnamon stick
- 1 small onion, sliced
- 4–5 cloves of garlic, crushed

A

- 1 cup fresh coconut milk
- Salt

BAGHAR

- 3 tbsp vegetable oil
- 2 tbsp sliced shallot
- 3–4 cloves of garlic, crushed
- 3–4 dry red chillies, coarsely ground with a little water
- 10–15 curry leaves

Sri Lanka is known for its spices—cloves, cinnamon, pepper, cardamom, nutmeg and mace—that are grown aplenty. It is, therefore, natural that Sri Lankans use them a lot in their cuisine, making it delicious and aromatic. Spices, coconut, shallots and red chillies are combined in this dish to give it a wonderful flavour.

. . . .

Wash and soak the lentils in 3–4 glasses of water for 30 minutes. Drain before cooking.

Put the lentils in a pressure cooker along with all the ingredients at 'A', three glasses of water and salt. Pressure cook till just 1 whistle, and then reduce the flame to low. Cook for another 2–3 minutes. Open the cooker when the pressure subsides. The lentils at this stage should be tender. If not, cook a little more, without the lid on, till the lentils are tender. Mash lightly. Add coconut milk and mix. Bring the lentils to a boil and then turn off the heat.

Separately heat oil in a sauce pan, and add the shallot. When the shallot turns pink, add the garlic. When shallot and garlic turn golden brown, add the red chillies, followed in a few seconds by curry leaves. After about 5–10 seconds, pour the baghar over the lentils and mix.

Serve hot with plain rice or/and bread.

Note: For Sri Lankan curry powder, see the next recipe.

SRI LANKAN CURRY POWDER

Sri Lankan raw curry powder is wonderfully aromatic blend of spices and is used in Sri Lankan cuisine in many varieties of dals and vegetables.

- 15-20 stems of curry leaves
- 50 g coriander seeds
- 30 g cumin seeds
- 1 tbsp fennel seeds
- 1 tbsp fenugreek seeds
- 1 cinnamon stick, about 3-inches long
- 1 tsp cloves
- 1 tsp cardamom seeds

Wash and shake dry the curry leaves. Remove the leaves from the stems.

Heat a heavy-bottom pan and lightly dry roast the curry leaves on medium flame till they are completely dry. Do not allow to brown. Remove and set aside.

Next, dry roast the coriander seeds, cumin seeds, fennel, fenugreek seeds, cinnamon, cloves and cardamom for just a minute or two till a nice aroma starts to come. Do not allow to brown. Remove and allow to cool.

Now grind together all the above ingredients to a fine powder.

Store in an air-tight jar. Will remain good for use for long.

MAA KI DAL, NEPALI-STYLE

PREPARATION TIME
20 minutes

COOKING TIME
30 minutes

SERVES
6

Black gram lentil or Urad dal was brought to India by Punjabis from the western part of Punjab, which is now in Pakistan. Dal Makhni, a rich version of this dal is cooked with loads of butter and cream. It is highly popular and an inseparable part of Indian cuisine.

Maa ki dal, Nepali-style is altogether a simple variety of urad dal. Easy to make, it is super delicious and a favourite in Nepal. The baghar of ghee and mustard oil impart a unique flavour to this dish which is further enhanced by liberal use of garlic and chillies, both red and green.

- 250 g black gram lentils, split and unskinned (urad dal, dali)
- 1/3rd tsp turmeric
- 1/2 tsp oil
- Salt

BAGHAR
- 2 tbsp ghee
- 2 tbsp mustard oil
- 6–7 dry red chillies, whole
- 5–6 green chillies whole, slit down the middle
- 1 tsp cumin seeds
- 1 pod garlic, chopped
- 1½ tsp red chilli powder
- 1 tsp dry coriander powder

Wash and pressure cook the lentils with salt, turmeric and ½ tsp oil in 3–4 glasses of water. After 2 whistles, lower the flame and let the lentils simmer for about 5–6 minutes. Turn off the flame. When the pressure subsides, check the lentils. They should be tender, but not overcooked. If need be cook them further without pressure on medium-low flame with a lid on.

Heat the ghee and oil together in a pan. Add the whole red chillies, green chillies and cumin seeds. After a few seconds, add the garlic. When the garlic turns golden brown, remove from the flame. Add the red chilli powder and coriander powder. Add this baghar to the lentils. Mix and cook covered for about 5 minutes.

The dish has medium-thin consistency. Goes well with both rice and roti.

Soups

SOUPS

Soups are comforting, easy to prepare and filling. They are not only nutritious as they contain minerals, vitamins, fibre and proteins but are also low in fat.

Soups feature in every cuisine around the world. Faki soup is a Greek lentil soup, with carrots, olive oil, herbs and tomatoes. Bird's Nest soup is a delicacy of Chinese cuisine. Minestrone is an Italian vegetable soup. Then there is the famous Miso soup made from fish broth and fermented soy in Japan. Mulligatawny - (an Anglo-Indian soup). In Tamil Nadu, India, the word Mulligatawny comes from the words mulliga, meaning 'pepper' and tanni which means 'water'. Rasam is a South Indian traditional soup where steamed lentils are used in conjunction with tamarind, pepper and cumin. Lentil soups are popular in Middle Eastern and Mediterranean cuisines.

Soups are generally served hot but cold soup such as Gazpacho, a Spanish soup, is made with tomato and grated cucumber or chilled cucumber, apple and mint, and can also be delightful on a hot summer day.

Almost any vegetable lends itself to use in soups. And they can be combined with meat, chicken or fish, or with shellfish such as prawns, lobsters or crabs to make the most flavoursome soups.

The addition of an attractive garnish, a sprinkling of herbs, crispy onions or shallots, a swirl of cream or a dash of cinnamon powder or pepper can magically enhance the flavour of soups.

I started making soups frequently after realizing that my daughter, Gauri, displayed a clear predilection for soups. She loves soups of all kinds—be it a broth or chunky vegetables with chicken, carrot and tomato soup. In fact, during a visit to Vietnam, I found all my family took to the Vietnamese soup Pho. They would have it with almost every meal.

A wholesome soup and a luscious salad can make a meal complete.

So, here in the next section are recipes of some legume-based soups to make your meals special.

A NOTE FROM MY DAUGHTER, GAURI

Since I was a child, my mother has nourished me, body and soul, with a variety of the most delicious and comforting soups. Whether a simple clear chicken soup or a more fancy minestrone or French onion soup, I can't remember enjoying a bowl of soup anywhere in the world as much as those made by my mother in the comfort of our home, with all her love and affection poured into it.

If ever I were asked what my favourite meal was, it's definitely my mother's soup. I've grown up having so much cream of tomato soup, carrot, pumpkin, gazpacho, Chinese hot and sour, lentil soups, mixed vegetable soups to say the least. And my mother still continues to look for more recipes to add to her repertoire. I relish them each and every time they're made.

I love soups for how delicious and wholesome (as my mother has always said) they are. To me, every soup is comfort for the soul. Being a health food fanatic, I love them for being rich in nutrients, light on the tummy yet filling, but I love them most because for me it's the association with my mother's cooking, how brilliantly she makes the simplest of things and with all of her heart and love for us.

When I come home after a long day, there's nothing more comforting than a warm bath, pajamas and a hearty and healthy bowl of soup made by my mother.

MASOOR DAL SOUP

PREPARATION TIME
5 minutes

COOKING TIME
20 minutes

SERVES
6

- 75 g red lentils (masoor dal)
- 4 tomatoes, chopped
- 1 onion, chopped
- 1 inch piece of ginger, crushed
- 3 cloves
- 1 bay leaf
- 10–15 curry leaves
- 1 green chilli, split down the middle

} X

- Juice of 1½–2 lime
- ¼th tsp white pepper powder
- A few sprigs of fresh green coriander, chopped
- Salt

This is a red lentil soup with flavours of ginger, green chilli, lime and fresh green coriander.

Wash and soak the lentils for 1 hour. Drain the water.

Place the lentils with all the ingredients at 'X', together with salt and 3½ glasses of water in a pressure cooker. Pressure cook till 2–3 whistles. Reduce the flame and cook further for 4–5 minutes. Open the lid once the pressure subsides. Mash and strain the lentils through a fine strainer. Heat the lentil stock and bring it to a boil.

Heat the soup well just before serving. Add the lime juice and white pepper. Serve in individual soup bowls, garnished with fresh green coriander.

MOONG DAL SOUP

PREPARATION TIME
10 minutes

COOKING TIME
20 minutes

SERVES
4–5

- 100 g green gram lentils, split and skinned (moong dal, dhuli)
- 2 medium onions, chopped
- 4 spring onions, chopped
- 1 potato, diced
- 1½ tbsp butter
- 1 tbsp celery, chopped
- 1 green chilli, split
- 1 tsp dill chopped
- ¼th tsp white pepper powder
- Salt

A light and invigorating soup with celery and dill adding an aromatic note.

Wash and soak the lentils in 2–3 glasses of water for 15–20 minutes. Drain the water and wash the lentils again.

Place the lentils along with half of the chopped onion, spring onion and potato in the pressure cooker. Add 4 glasses of water and pressure cook till 2–3 whistles. Lower the heat and cook for another 2–3 minutes. Open when the pressure subsides. When slightly cool, blend in a blender and strain through a fine sieve. Now, the stock is ready.

Heat butter in a heavy-base pan. Add the remaining chopped onion, spring onion, celery and the green chilli, and sauté for a minute. Add the stock and bring to a boil. Simmer for 2 minutes. Add dill, salt and pepper, and simmer for another 2–3 minutes.

Serve piping hot in individual soup bowls.

KIDNEY BEAN SOUP

PREPARATION TIME
10 minutes

COOKING TIME
30 minutes

SERVES
6

- 150 g red kidney
  beans (rajma)
- 5 tomatoes
- 2 tbsp olive oil
- 1 large onion,
  chopped
- 1 inch piece of ginger,
  crushed
- 3 garlic cloves,
  crushed
- 2 fresh red chillies
- 2–3 spring onions,
  chopped
- 1 tbsp fresh coriander,
  chopped
- A few drops of
  Tabasco sauce
- ¼th tsp white pepper
  powder
- Wedges of 1 lime
- Salt

This is a simple and delicious soup. Tabasco, lime and white pepper give this kidney bean soup the extra zest.

Wash and soak the kidney beans in 4 glasses of water overnight or at least for 5–6 hours before cooking. Drain the water and wash the kidney beans again.

Wash and plunge the tomatoes into boiling water for 1–2 minutes. Remove them and run under cold water for a few seconds. Peel off the skin and chop roughly. Set aside.

Heat oil in a pressure cooker. Add the onion, ginger, garlic and the fresh red chillies, and sauté for 1–2 minutes. Add tomatoes and salt, and sauté for another 5 minutes. Add kidney beans, 4½ glasses of water and pressure cook till 3 whistles. Reduce the flame and cook further for 8–10 minutes. Open the pressure cooker when the steam subsides.

Remove half a cup of kidney beans and set aside. After they have cooled a bit, lightly blend the kidney beans in a blender. Press through a fine sieve to get kidney beans stock.

Heat the stock in a heavy-base pan and bring to a boil. Add the kidney beans kept aside earlier as well as the spring onions. Simmer for 5 minutes. Add fresh coriander, a few drops of Tabasco sauce, and the white pepper powder. Simmer for another minute.

Serve piping hot in individual soup bowls, garnished with wedges of lime.

CHICKPEA AND RED LENTIL SOUP

PREPARATION TIME
10 minutes

COOKING TIME
30 minutes

SERVES
6

- 50 g chickpeas (Kabuli chana)
- 50 g red lentils (masoor dal)
- 6 tomatoes
- 1 tbsp butter
- 1 tbsp oil
- 1 onion, chopped
- 1 tbsp fresh coriander, chopped
- 1 tbsp fresh parsley, chopped
- 2 fresh red chillies, chopped
- ¼th tsp cinnamon powder
- ¼th tsp white pepper powder
- Salt

GARNISH
- A few fresh coriander leaves
- 1 lime, sliced
- A sprinkling of cinnamon powder

Soups made with lentils are nutritious and delicious. This is a rich and satisfying chickpeas and red lentil soup with fragrant herbal flavours of parsley and fresh coriander.

Wash and soak the chickpeas in 2 glasses of water overnight. Drain the water. Wash the chickpeas again.

Wash and soak the red lentils in 1 glass of water for 30 minutes. Drain the water. Wash the lentils again.

Plunge the tomatoes in boiling water for 1 minute. Remove and run them under cold water. Peel off the skin and chop roughly. Set aside.

Heat the butter and oil in a pressure cooker. Add the chopped onion and sauté for 30 seconds. Add the drained chickpeas, red lentils, tomatoes, fresh coriander, parsley, red chillies and cinnamon powder. Cook for about 8–10 minutes. Add 4 glasses of water and pressure cook till 2–3 whistles. Reduce the heat to low and cook further for 5–10 minutes. Open when the pressure subsides.

Add salt and white pepper and cook for another 2–3 minutes.

Ladle piping-hot soup into individual soup bowls and garnish with coriander, lime slices and a sprinkling of cinnamon.

CHICKPEA SOUP WITH VEGETABLES

PREPARATION TIME
15–20 minutes

COOKING TIME
40 minutes

SERVES
6

- 100 g chickpeas (Kabuli chana)
- 3 tomatoes
- 1½ tbsp oil
- 2–3 spring onions or 1 leek, chopped coarsely
- 1 stick celery, chopped coarsely
- 1 carrot, sliced round
- 1 medium-sized potato, diced
- 50 g spinach, chopped
- 50 g cabbage, chopped
- 4 cloves garlic, crushed
- 1 bay leaf
- ¼th tsp black pepper powder
- ¼th tsp white pepper powder
- Salt

Chickpeas have an earthy richness. Chickpeas, herbs and vegetables combine to make this a refreshing, healthy and fragrant soup.

Wash and soak the chickpeas overnight. Drain the water and wash again.

Boil the chickpeas in 4–4 ½ glasses of water in a pressure cooker till 2–3 whistles. Reduce heat to low and cook for another 10 minutes. Open the pressure cooker when the steam subsides. The chickpeas should be tender. Remove 25 g of chickpeas and keep aside.

Wash and plunge the tomatoes in boiling water for 1 minute. Remove and run them under cold water. Peel off the skin and chop roughly. Set aside.

Heat the oil in a heavy-base pan. Add the spring onions or leek, celery, carrot, potato, spinach, garlic and bay leaf, as well as the blanched tomatoes.

Cover and cook for 10 minutes. Add the previously boiled chickpeas (with the water in which they were boiled), pepper and salt, and cook on medium-low flame for about 10–12 minutes till well blended. This soup should be of medium thickness.

Serve piping hot with crusty bread.

BLACK-EYED BEAN SOUP

PREPARATION TIME
10 minutes

COOKING TIME
30 minutes

SERVES
5–6

- 100 g black-eyed beans (lobia)
- 4 tomatoes
- 1 tbsp olive or vegetable oil
- 1 large onion, chopped
- 4 garlic cloves, chopped
- 1–2 green chillies, chopped
- ¾th tsp cumin, ground
- 2 tbsp fresh coriander, chopped
- Juice of 1 lime
- Salt

A quick and simple soup. Fresh lime gives it just the right zest.

Wash and soak the lobia fully covered with water, for 1 hour. Drain and place them in a pressure cooker.

Add 4 glasses of water and pressure cook till 3 whistles. Reduce the heat to low and cook further for 8–10 minutes. Remove from flame. Open when the pressure subsides. The lobia should be tender. If not cook a little more with the lid off.

Wash and plunge the tomatoes into boiling water for 1 minute. Remove and run them under cold water. Peel off the skin and chop roughly. Set aside.

Heat the oil in a heavy-base pan. Add the chopped onion and garlic. When the onion turns translucent, add the green chillies and cook for 2–3 minutes.

Add tomatoes, cumin powder and half of the fresh coriander and salt. Cook for about 10 minutes. Now add the previously boiled lobia with the water in which it was boiled. Bring the dish to a boil. Lower heat and simmer for 10 minutes. Turn off the flame. Add the remaining coriander and juice of fresh lime.

Ladle hot into individual soup bowls.

SPICY CHICKPEA SOUP

PREPARATION TIME
15 minutes

COOKING TIME
30 minutes

SERVES
5–6

- 100 g chickpeas (Kabuli chana)
- 4–5 tomatoes
- 2 tbsp olive oil
- 1 onion, chopped
- 1 tbsp grated ginger
- 1 carrot, diced
- 1 potato, diced
- 1 small celery stick, chopped
- 1 green chilli
- 1 fresh red chilli
- 2 tbsp fresh coriander, chopped
- ½ tsp freshly ground black pepper
- 2–3 spring onions, chopped
- Wedges of 1 lime, fried crisp
- Salt

Spicy and vibrant, this soup combines the flavours of hearty and healthy vegetables with the naturally earthy flavour of chickpeas. Green chilli, red chilli and pepper give it a punch and take this soup to another level.

Wash and soak the chickpeas overnight in 3 glasses of water. Drain the water.

Wash the chickpeas again and pressure cook in 4½ glasses of water till 2–3 whistles. Reduce the flame and cook further for 10 minutes. Open once the pressure subsides. The chickpeas at this stage should be tender. Remove about 25 g of chickpeas and set aside. Strain the chickpeas and keep the chickpeas and stock separately.

Wash and plunge the tomatoes in boiling water for 1–2 minutes. Remove and run cold water over them. Peel off the skin and chop roughly. Set aside.

Take a heavy-bottom pan. Heat the oil and stir in the onion. Once the onion turns translucent, add the ginger and tomatoes. Also add carrot, potato, celery, green chilli, red chilli, half of the fresh coriander, and pepper and salt. Simmer gently for 6–7 minutes.

Now add the previously cooked chickpeas, chopped spring onions and cook on a medium flame for 2–3 minutes. Then add the stock and bring the dish to a boil. Reduce the flame to medium-low and simmer for 6–7 minutes.

Serve hot, speckled with the remaining coriander and crispy fried lime wedges.

MASOOR DAL SOUP
WITH VEGETABLES

PREPARATION TIME
10–15 minutes

COOKING TIME
30 minutes

SERVES
6–8

- 150 g red lentils (masoor dal)
- 4 tomatoes (about 300 g), chopped
- 1 carrot, diced
- 70 g cabbage, chopped
- 50 g french beans, chopped
- 1 medium sized onion, chopped
- 1 tbsp ginger, grated
- 5–7 peppercorn, whole

A

- 3–4 spring onions, chopped
- 2 green chillies, each hand broken in 2
- A few sprigs of fresh green coriander, chopped
- Wedges of 3 limes
- Salt

Lentils together with vegetables, spring onions, green chillies and fresh green coriander result in a finely balanced combination of flavours. A simple but nutritious soup, at once soothing and comforting.

Wash and soak the lentils in 3 glasses of water for 20 minutes. Drain the water.

Place the lentils in a pressure cooker with 4 glasses of water, salt and all the ingredients of 'A'. Pressure cook till 2 whistles. Reduce the flame and cook further for 2 minutes. Open the lid when the pressure subsides.

Mash the boiled lentils and vegetables and strain through a sieve.

Transfer the soup to a heavy-base pan. Bring it to a boil. Now add the spring onions, green chillies and fresh green coriander. Cook for just about 1–2 minutes.

Ladle piping hot soup into individual soup bowls with lime wedges on the side.

ACKNOWLEDGEMENTS

There is nothing more precious in life than the love of your family and friends. It can help you realize your dreams and the unattainable becomes possible.

This venture of mine, *The Book of Dals*, just proves that. Though I started work on this book 3–4 years back, it was progressing with hiccups. On-again and off-again, I felt really pressured and almost guilty for not working on it fast. My grandson Azaan, then nine years old, asked me seriously, 'Gramia, why don't you finish your book?' The directness and sincerity of his remark hit me deep and I told him, 'I will.'

Then again my daughter, Nainika, told me strongly and pleadingly, 'Mamma, why don't you just finish this book, and stop going to office and working in the garden or the kitchen? In fact, you should stop doing all these things and write many more beautiful books. You will always be remembered and would have made an abiding contribution to the culinary world.'

Our close friend Peter Burleigh, the former US ambassador to India, is passionate about food and has always loved the food cooked in our home. He was so happy and excited when he found that I was working on this book. He would send me a lot of literature and articles on the subject, and exhort and nudge me to quickly finish the project. When he found that I was just not progressing, he in exasperation said, he won't nudge me again. That's when he nudged me the most. I am grateful to him for the support and encouragement he always gives.

My husband, Vijay Karan, has always encouraged me to take that one extra step, beyond me. He always says, 'You can do it!' And he has succeeded with me, pitching in every possible way. My earlier two books and now this one, as many other things in my life, are a result of his ceaseless efforts to make me do better than my best.

And my son, Gaurav, literally bombarded me with every possible information on lentils. He was always ready to do the research, computer savvy that he is and which I am not, and to help me in every possible way. Till the book went to the press, he stood by me like a rock. My dependence on him was huge. My daughter, Gauri, is a perfectionist. She is not only the official taster of my food but has always been the official editor of everything written at our home, including this book.

Gauri and Nainika, both, are naturally talented and are amazing with their creative designs. They worked unbelievably hard during the photoshoot of the book and contributed beautifully to the photography and food styling, clearly leaving their imprint and enhancing the quality of the book.

My thoughts go to my mother, Pushpawati, who was a splendid cook and could create miraculous food with little on hand. She initiated me, early in life, into the enticing and wonderful realm of cuisine.

Vijay Karan's mother, Jayanti Rani, was also a legendary cook. Even her vegetarian food was so popular that on Fridays, friends and relatives flocked to our home in Banjara Hills in Hyderabad to devour her specialities like the famous Khatti Dal, Baghare Baigan and lots more. They would even bring their tiffins to take the leftovers home. After my marriage, she was the first person I started pestering to teach me about Hyderabad cuisine. At some point, she would tire of me and say, 'Ab bas karo, mujhe ab radio sunne do.' Vijay Karan's older sister, Mummy Jia, whose cooking was particularly loved by my husband, also shared her knowledge of cooking ungrudgingly. I also thank Gita and Neena, my sisters-in-law, who were always there for me.

My friends—Kunda Mahurkar and Anita Taneja—graciously shared their knowledge of recipes from Maharashtra and Gujarat with me. I thank them both.

My thanks go to Shyam and Mandal, our domestic help, who were there at every step to help me with the book. My personal secretary, K.C. Das, helped me greatly in preparing the text. My special thanks go to Abhishek Misra and Tarim, who helped me complete this book smoothly.

Finally, I would like to acknowledge my publisher, Penguin Random House, with gratitude. Milee Ashwarya was the editor when my last book, *Biryani*, which was published by Random House in 2009. Since then, she goaded me on to write yet another book. And here we are with *The Book of Dals*. Milee, now the publisher of Penguin Random House, and her brilliant team have always been a source of encouragement and strength. Gurveen Chadha, the editor, has been positive all through the process and worked hard to take this book to the press. Sanchita Mukherjee, the brilliant, young book designer, has been simply amazing with the book design.

GLOSSARY

Bengal Gram Lentils, Whole	Kala Chana
Black Gram Lentils	Urad Dal
Black Gram Lentils, Split and Skinned	Urad Dal, Dhuli
Black Gram Lentils, Split and Unskinned	Urad Dal, Dali
Black Gram Lentils, Whole	Urad Dal, Sabut
Black-Eyed Beans	Lobia
Split Chickpeas or Bengal Gram Lentils, Split and Skinned	Chana Dal
Chickpeas	Kabuli Chana
Dry Pea Lentils	Matar
Green Gram Lentils, Split and Skinned	Moong Dal, Dhuli
Green Gram Lentils, Unskinned and Split	Moong Dal, Dali
Green Gram Lentils, Whole	Moong Dal, Sabut
Ochre Lentils, Whole	Masoor Dal, Sabut
Orange or Pink Lentils, Also Known as Red Lentils, Split and Skinned	Masoor Dal, Dhuli
Red Gram Lentils	Arhar Dal
Red Kidney Beans	Rajma

Split and Skinned Lentils	Dhuli Dal
Split and Unskinned Lentils	Dali Dal
Whole Lentils	Sabut Dal

Aniseed	Saunf
Asafoetida	Hing
Black Salt	Kala Namak
Blend of Ground Spices	Garam Masala
Bottle Gourd	Lauki
Caraway Seeds	Shah Jeera
Cauliflower	Gobhi
Clarified Butter	Ghee
Coriander Seed	Dhaniya ke Beej
Coriander	Hara Dhaniya
Cumin	Jeera
Date	Khajoor
Dried Whole Milk	Khoya
Drumsticks	Moonge ki Phalli

Dry Ginger Powder	Sonth
Dry Mango Powder	Amchoor
Fenugreek	Methi
Flatbread, Fried with Oil	Parantha
Flatbread, Puffy and Made of Flour	Kulcha
Flatbread, Usually Made with Flour	Naan
Flatbread, Usually Made with Wheat	Roti
Garlic	Lasun or Lassan
Gram Flour	Besan
Green Bottle Gourd	Kaddu or Ghia
Jaggery	Gur
Leafy Vegetable	Saag
Minced Meat, Usually Lamb Meat	Keema
Potato	Aloo
Purslane Leaves	Kulfa
Refined Flour	Maida
Scewpine Water	Kewda
Semolina	Suji
Silver Leaf	Chandi ke Varq
Spinach	Palak
Tamarind	Imli

Tomato	**Tamater**
Turmeric	**Haldi**
Turnip	**Shalgam**
Wafer	**Papad**
Wheat/Whole Wheat Flour	**Atta**
White Raddish	**Mooli**

INDEX

ABOUT THE AUTHOR

Pratibha Karan was born in Bombay and grew up in Bombay, Calcutta, Himachal Pradesh and Delhi. She did her MA (economics) from Lady Shri Ram College, Delhi University and then joined the IAS in 1967. As an IAS officer she has worked in Delhi, Pondicherry, Arunachal Pradesh and Central Government Ministries and held several key positions. She retired as Secretary, Ministry of Food Processing Industries, Government of India in 2003. She has authored two books—*A Princely Legacy: Hyderabadi Cuisine* and *Biryani*. Both these books are bestsellers and have received much critical acclaim and continue to sell well.

Her marriage to Vijay Karan, former Commissioner of Police, Delhi, and former Director, CBI, brought her face to face with Hyderabadi cuisine to which she took an instant and passionate fondness.

A Princely Legacy: Hyderabadi Cuisine was published by HarperCollins Publishers, India in 1998. This book is an articulation of an intensely precious culinary and cultural experience and takes you on a short and somewhat sentimental journey to Hyderabad.

The book *Biryani* was published by Random House India in 2009. Immaculately researched, full of extraordinary recipes and beautifully designed and photographed, *Biryani* is an all-encompassing book on this princely dish.

The Book of Dals is her third book.